Fear No More
An Adult Coloring Book Of Bible Verses On Overcoming Fear

By
Ethlyn MacDonald

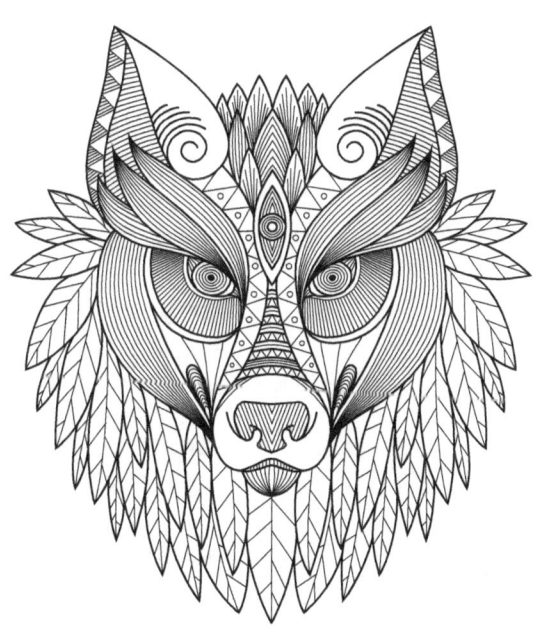

Edited By Katie Russell
Copyright © 2017
Improve and Impact, Inc.
All rights reserved.

ISBN: 1975813820

ISBN-13: 978-1975813826

ABOUT THE DESIGN OF MY COLORING BOOKS

COMPLEXITY: When I was facing cancer and going through chemotherapy, I renewed my interest in coloring. I was frustrated by trying to find coloring books that had different levels of complexity and styles. I design my books for a variety of coloring enthusiasts.

-A third of the designs are complex,
-A third of the designs are medium complexity.
-A third of the designs are simpler for when you want to color but you have less time and don't want an overwhelming project to complete.

It is my hope that by providing a multitude of complexity and design styles, coloring can be fun, therapeutic, and frustration free for all!

BLOTTING PAGES: At the end of the book you will find blotting pages. When self-publishing, Independent authors are not given a choice of paper thickness nor given the option of perforating the pages for easy Removal. Possibly in the future, the printers will let us have those Features because we know how important they are.

The blotting pages should help you to be able to use markers if you so Compendium Of Included Designs
desire without ruining the pages underneath. Simply remove one and slip it underneath the design.

You can also use the pages to test and keep track of your color choices. No more losing your test scrap paper before you complete your design and having to guess which color you used! I hate that! If you are the
artistic type, feel free to use the space for designs of your own!

**IF YOU ENJOYED MY BOOK, PLEASE LEAVE A REVIEW!
I AM AN INDEPENDANT AUTHOR & ILLUSTRATOR. POSITIVE REVIEWS
HELP OTHERS TO FIND MY BOOKS ONLINE!
THANK YOU FROM THE BOTTOM OF MY HEART!**

Compendium Of Included Designs

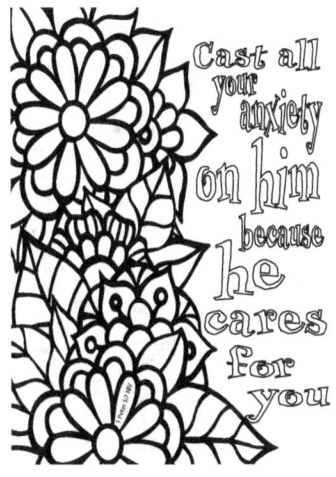
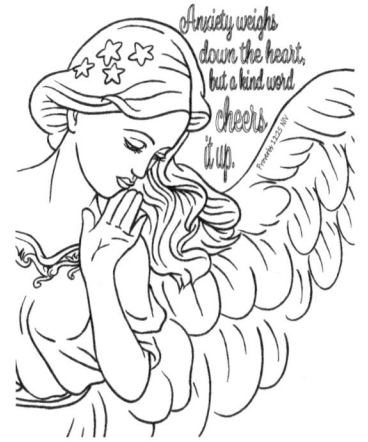
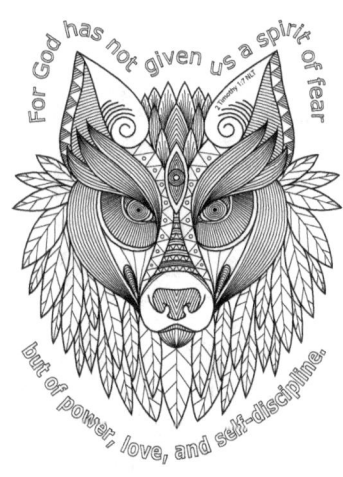
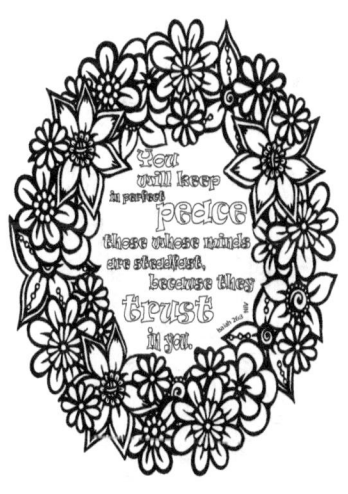
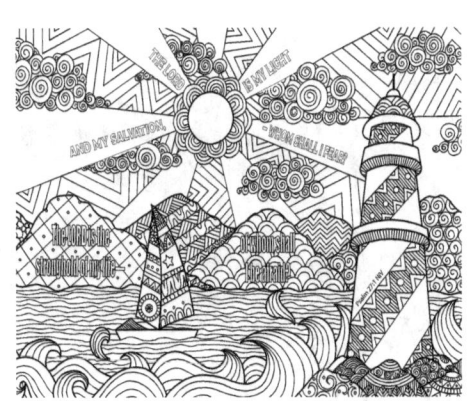
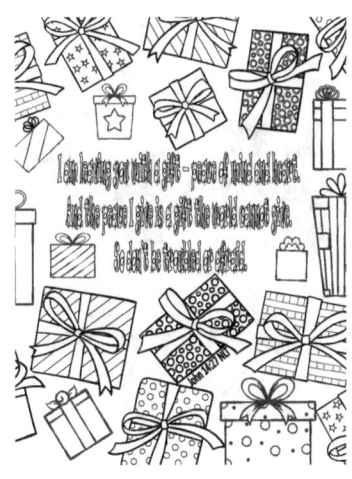

Compendium Of Included Designs

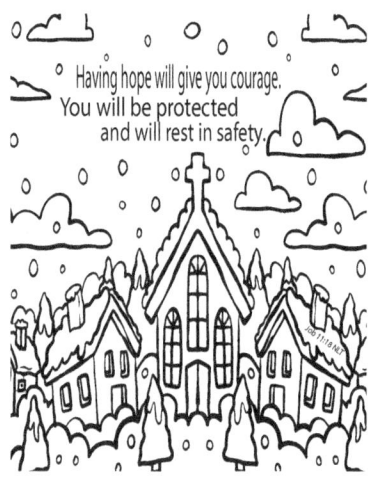
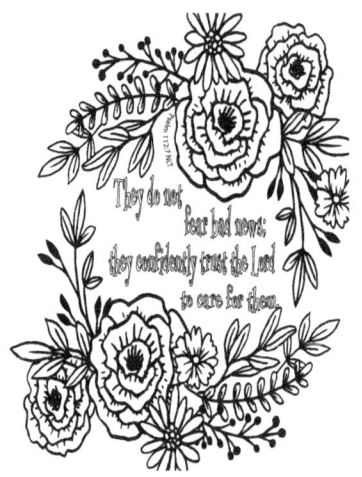
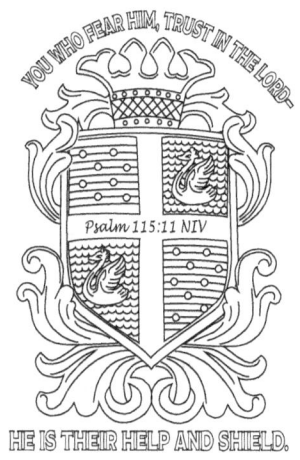
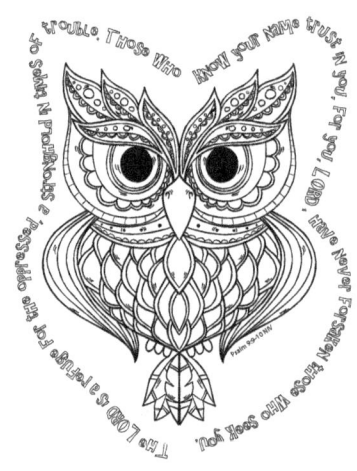
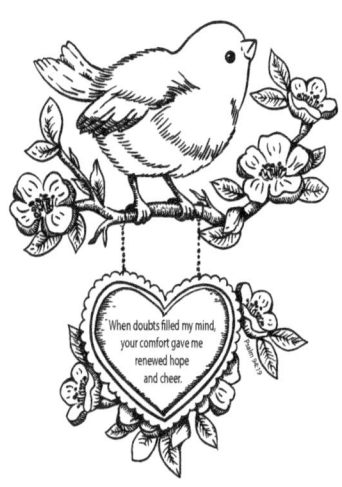
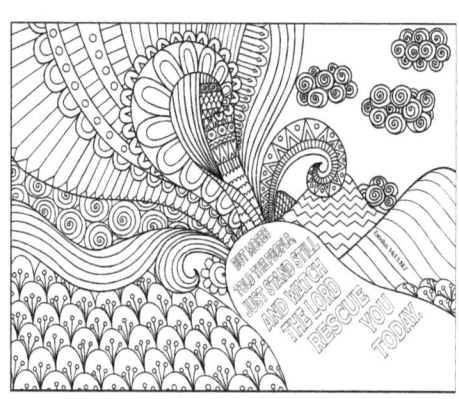

Compendium Of Included Designs

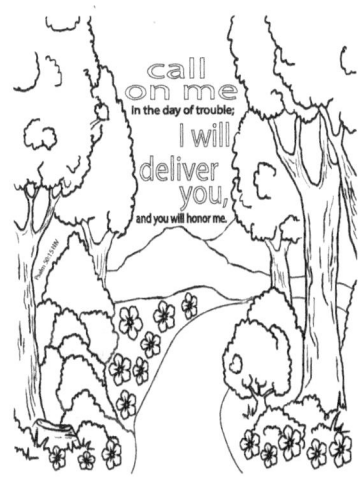
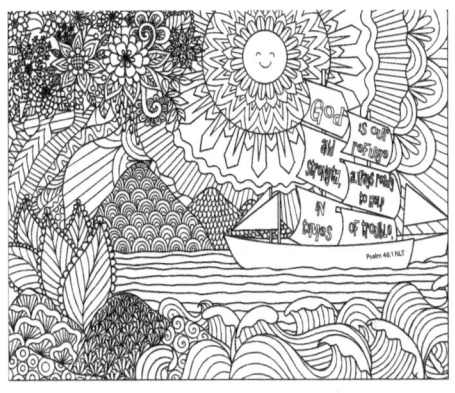
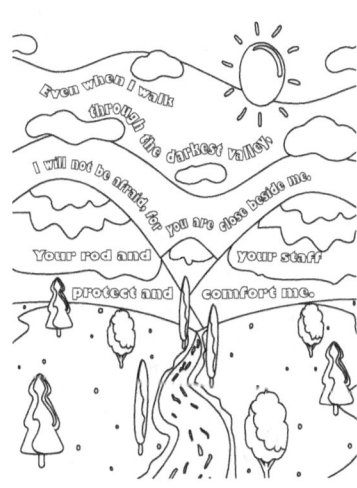
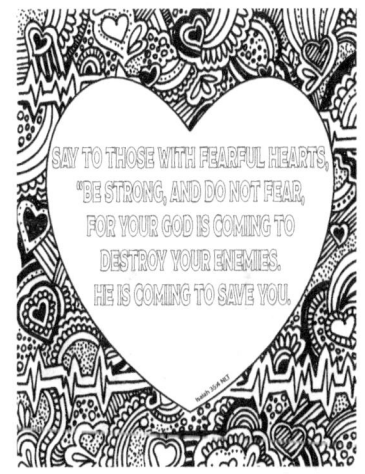
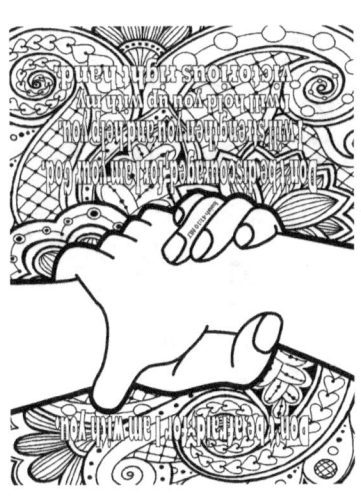
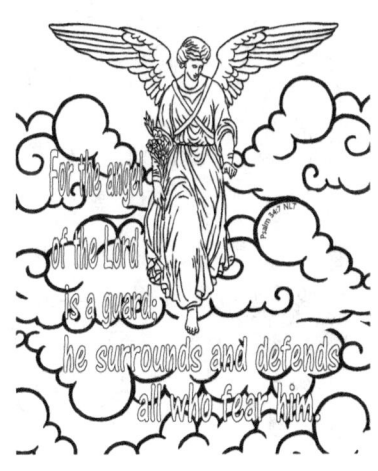

Compendium Of Included Designs

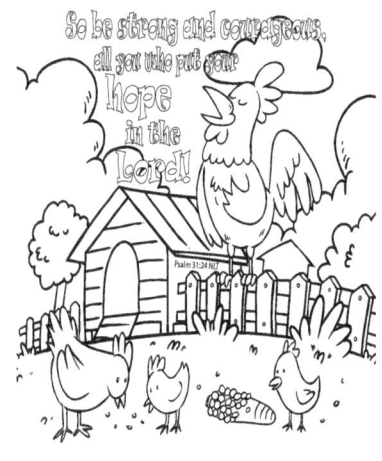
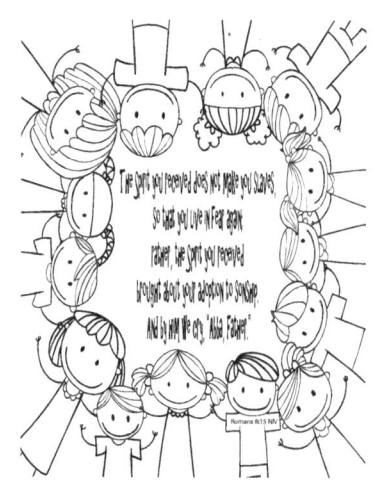
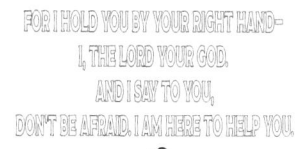
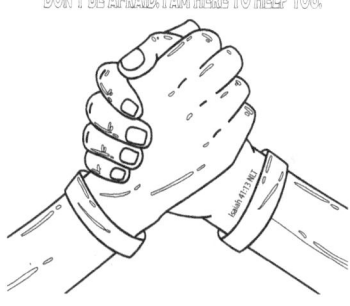
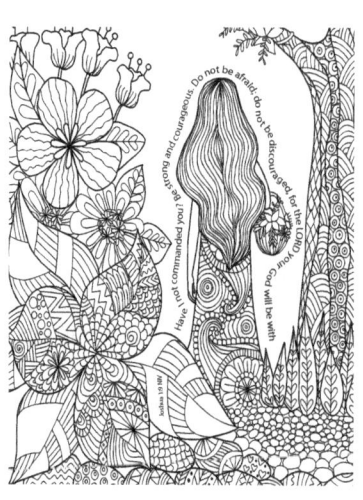
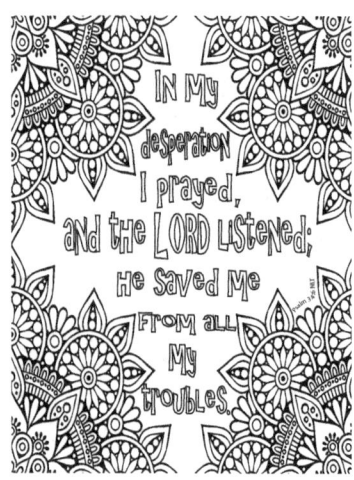
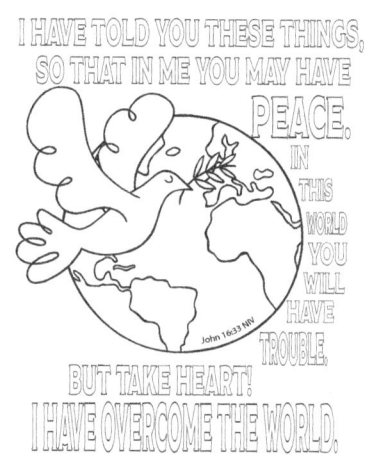

Compendium Of Included Designs

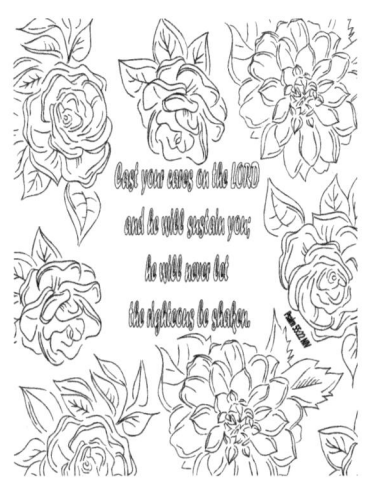
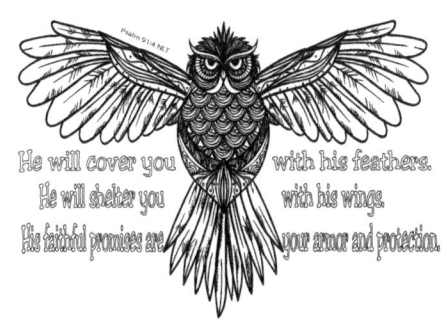
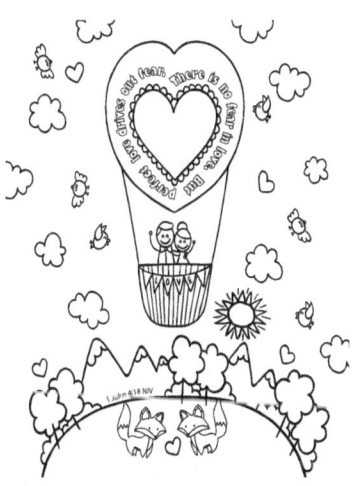
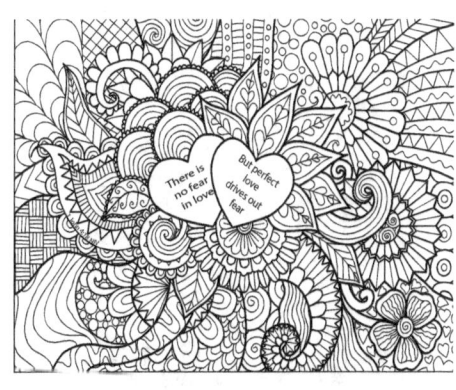
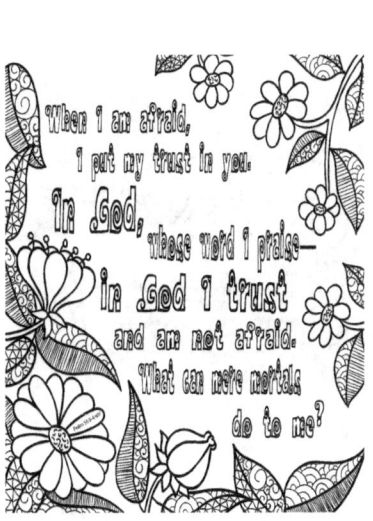
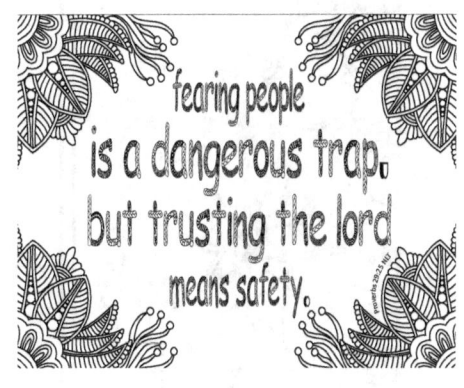

Compendium Of Included Designs

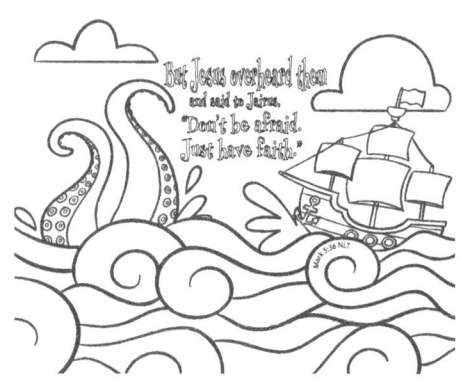
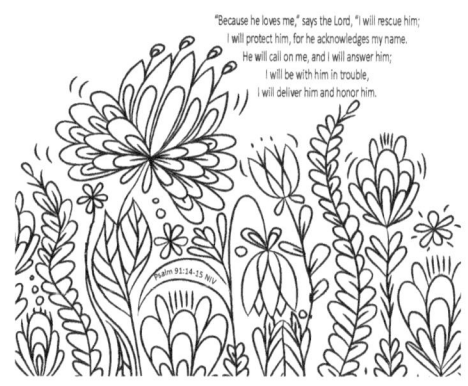
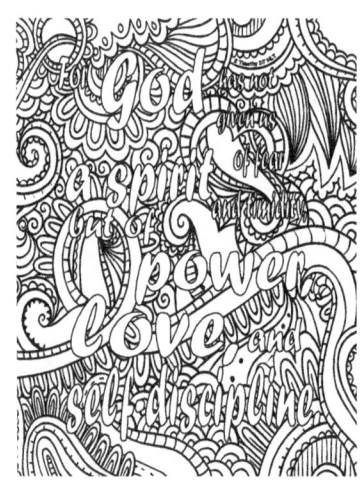
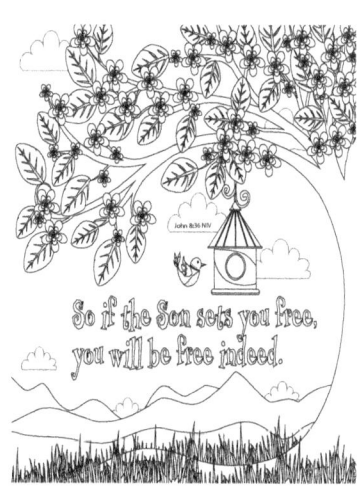
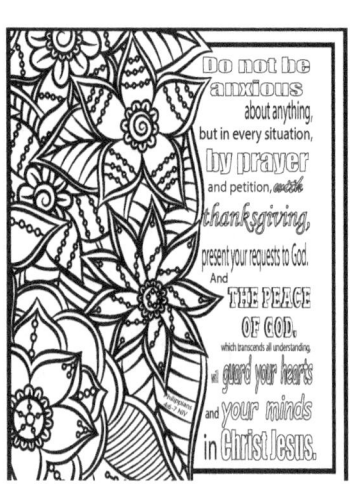
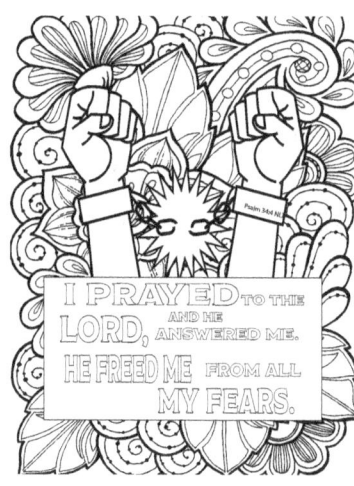

Compendium Of Included Designs

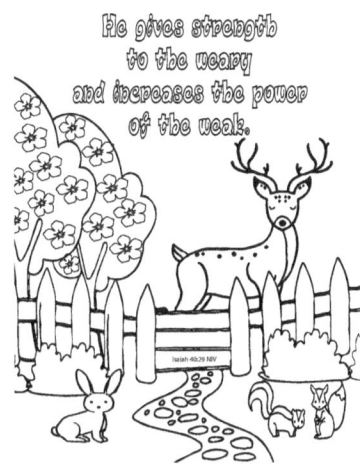
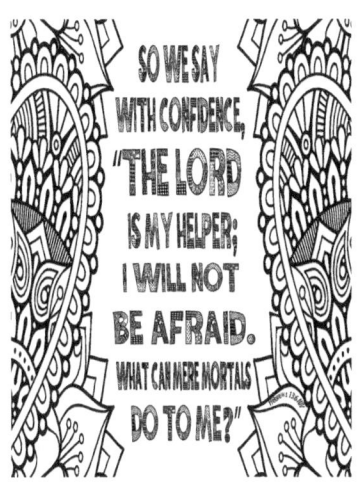
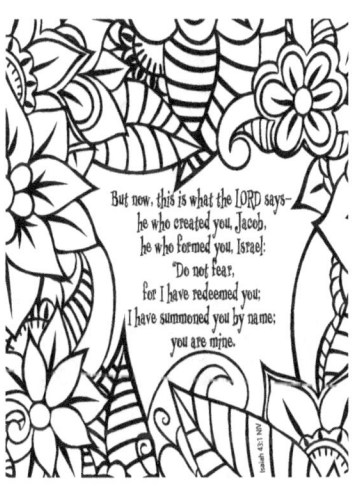
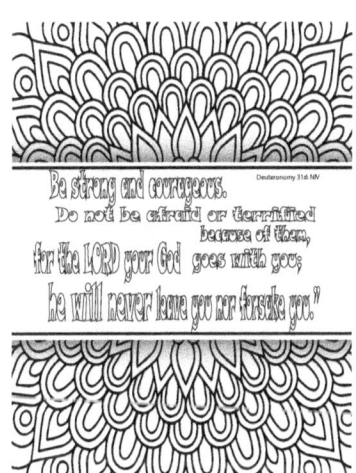

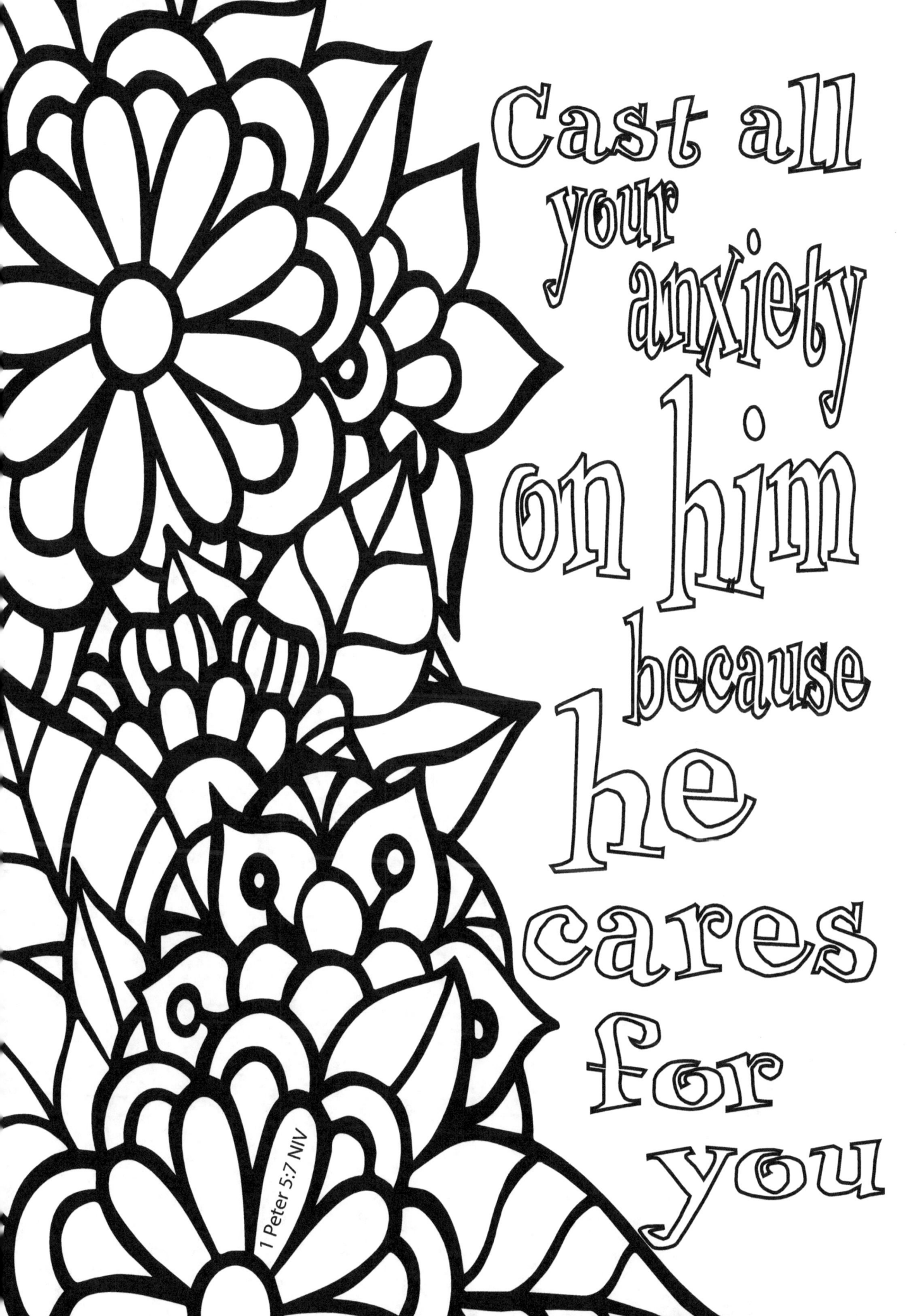

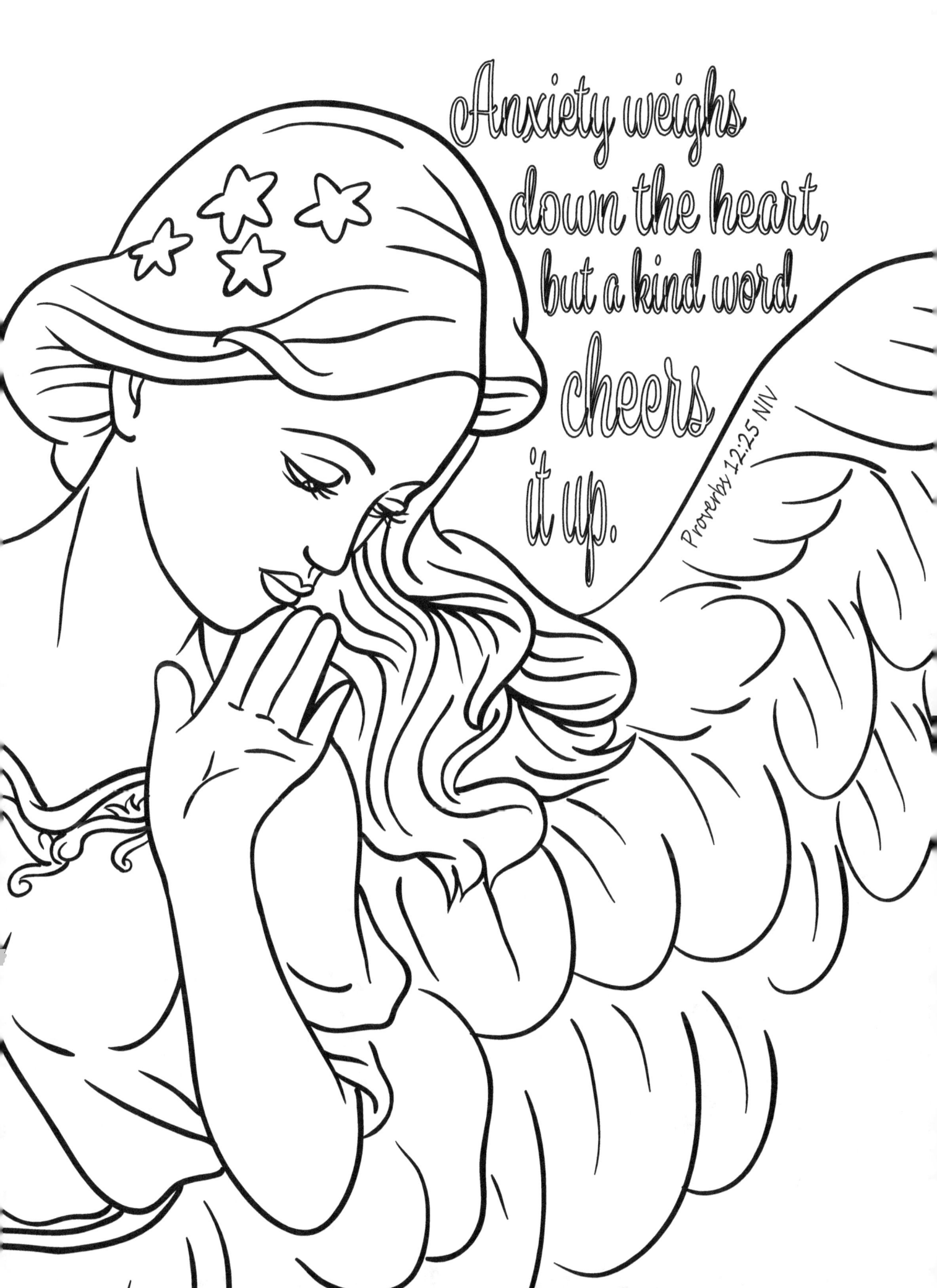

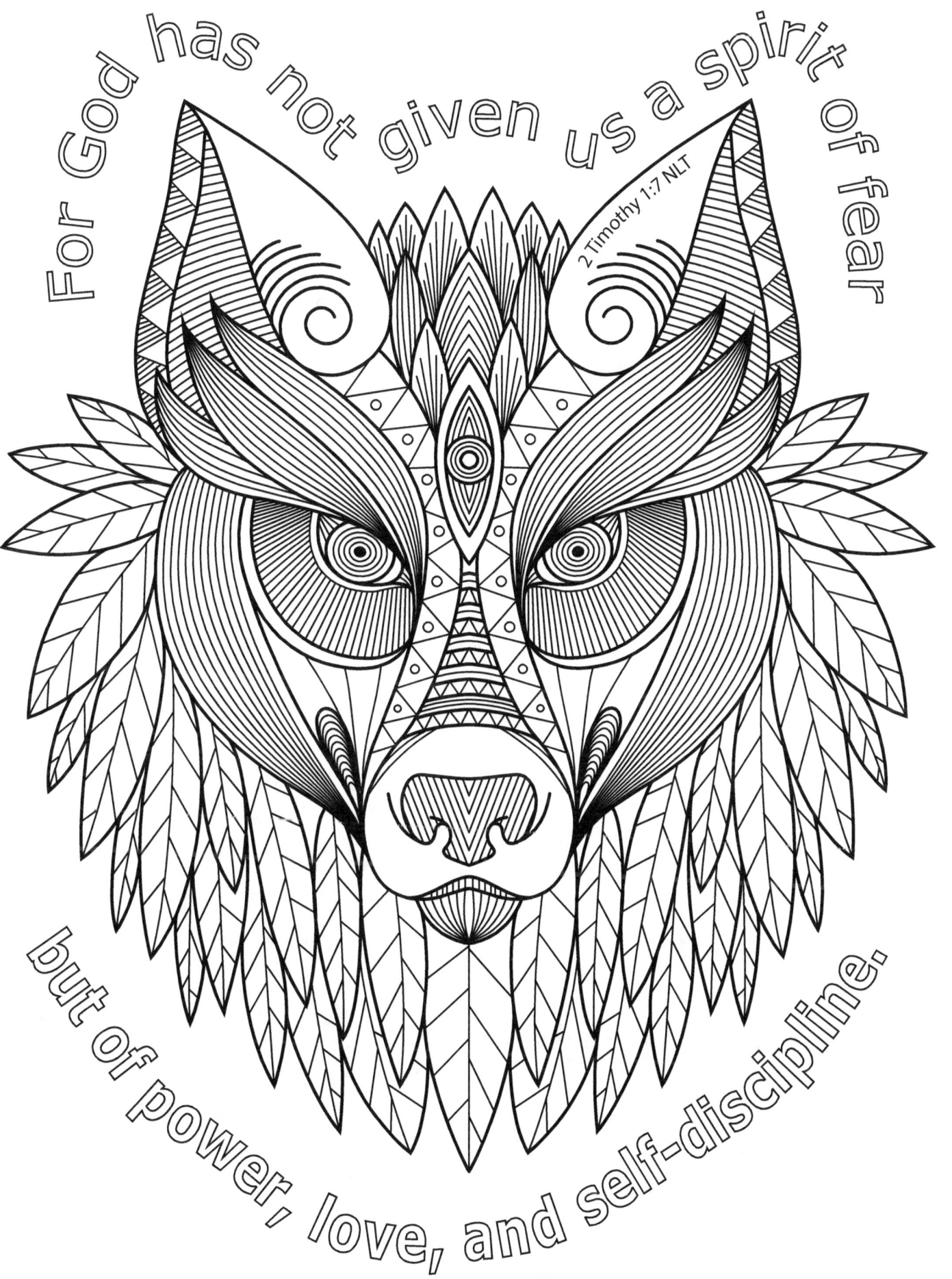

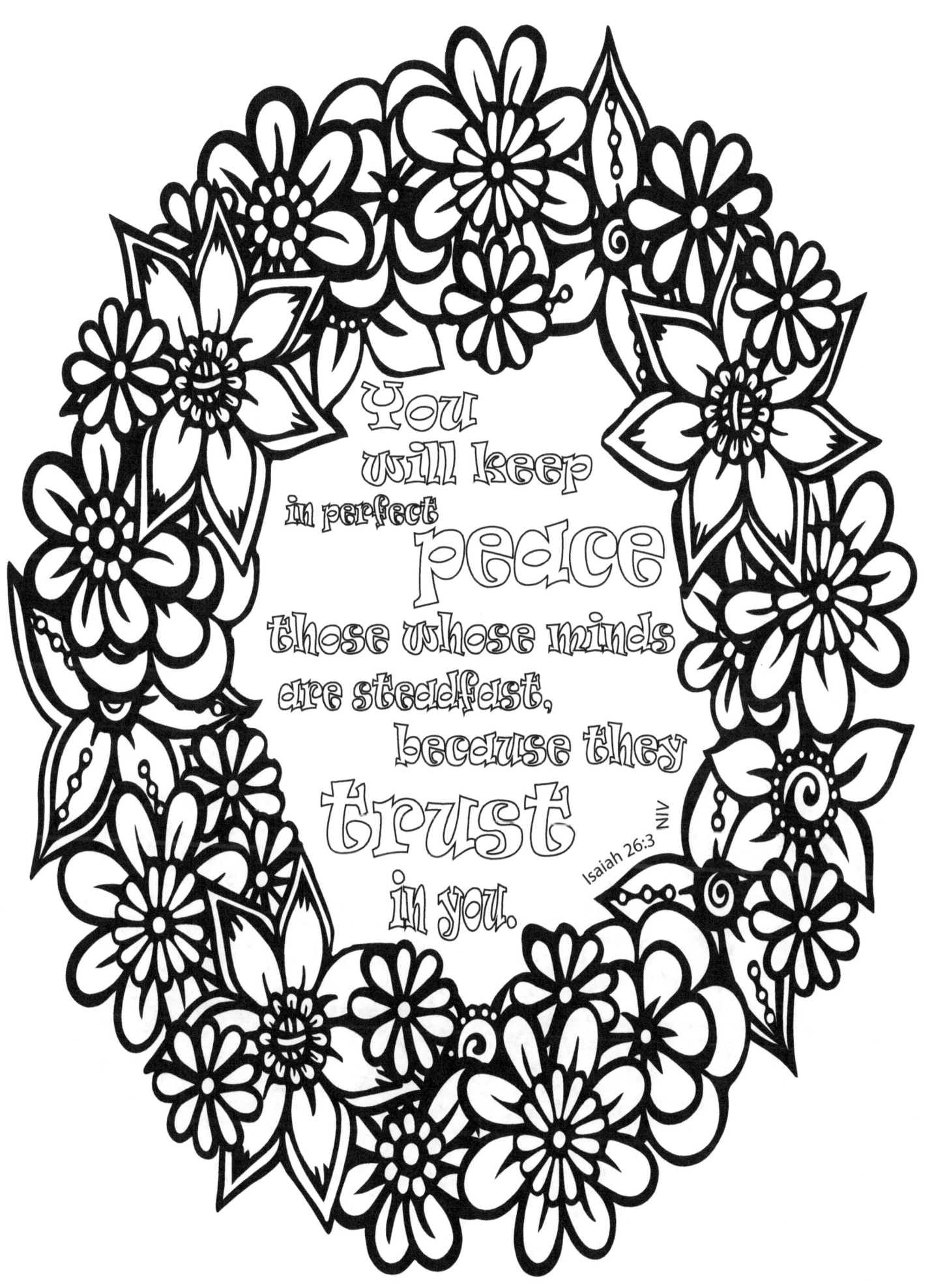

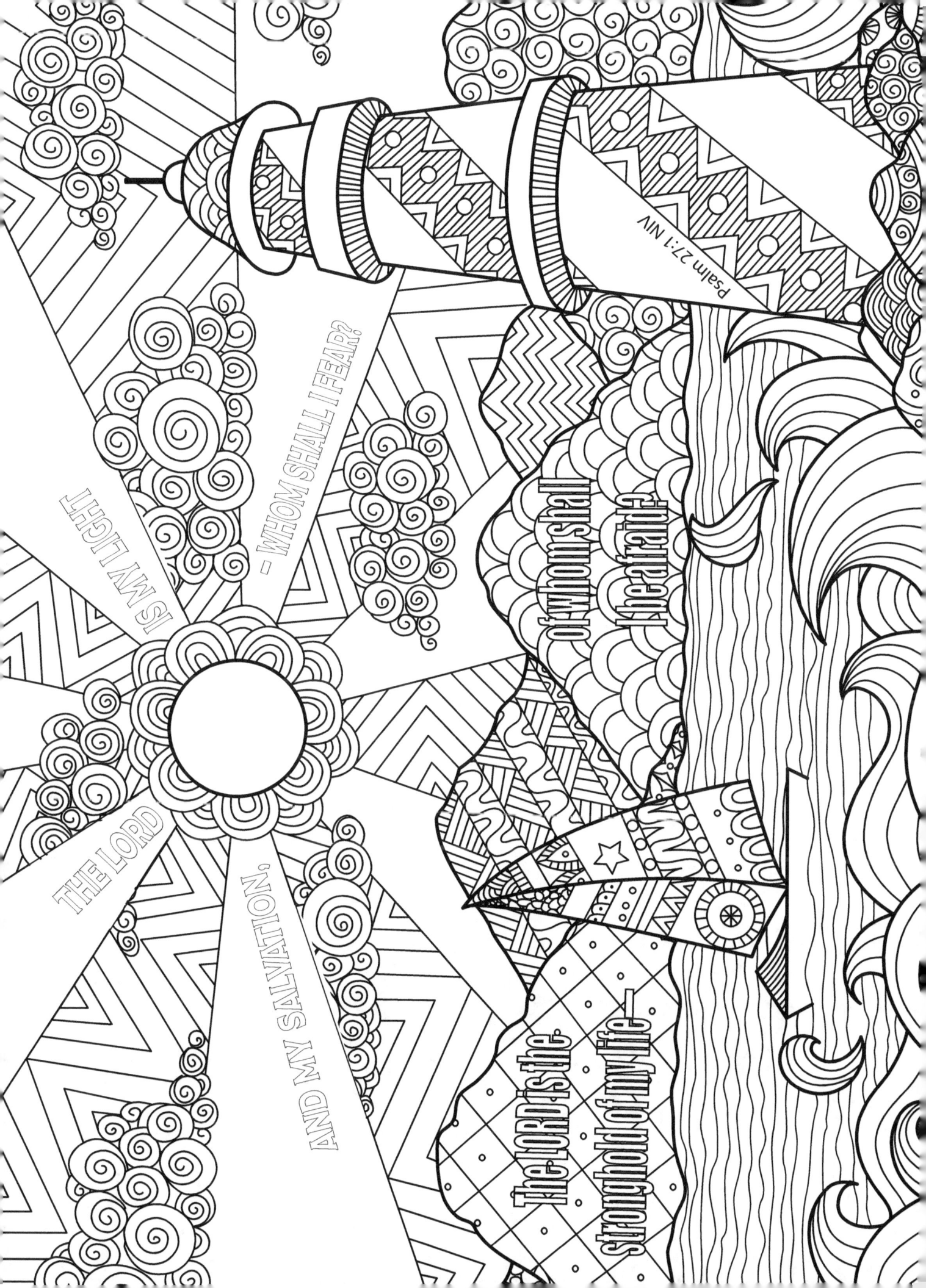

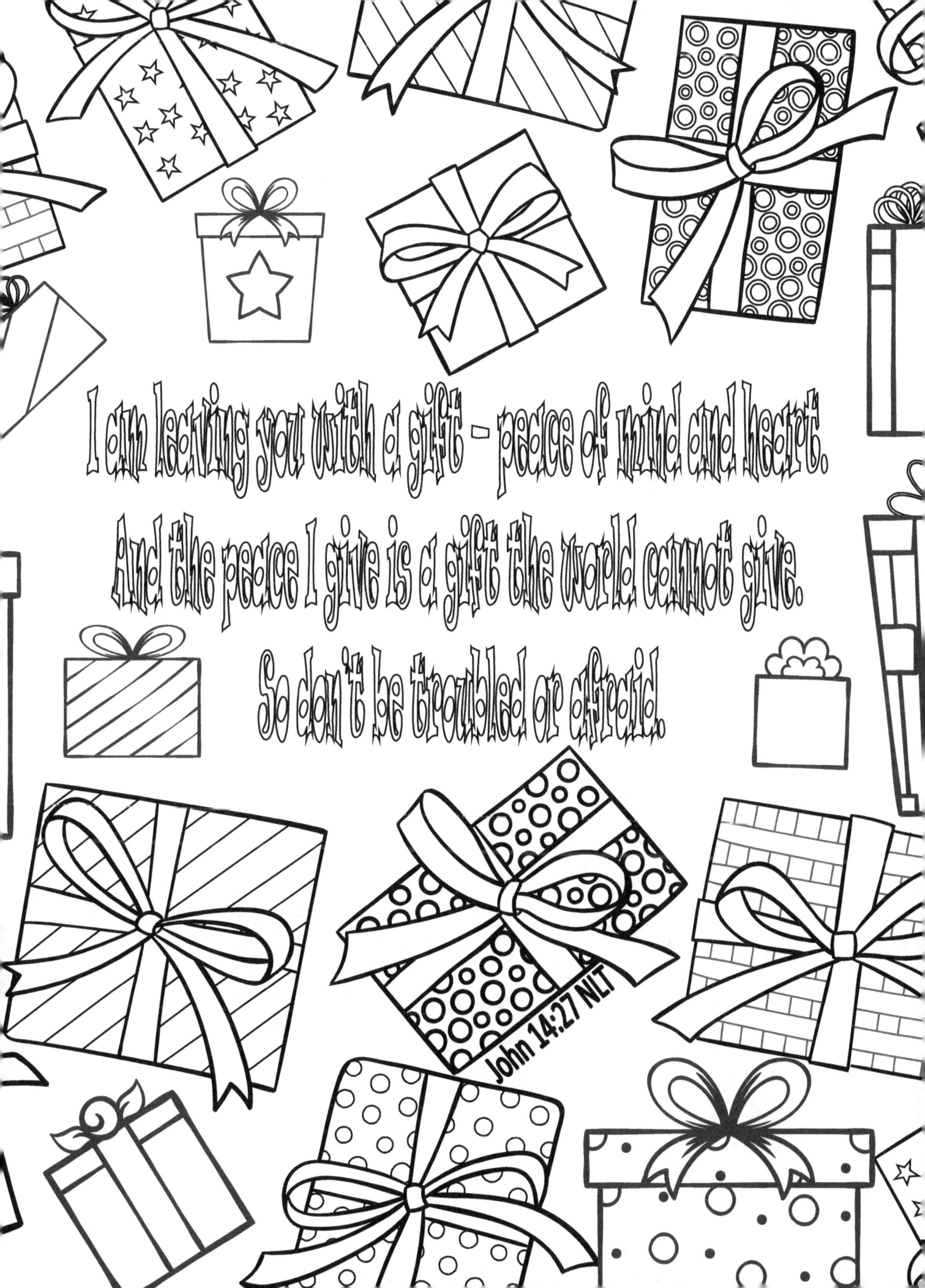

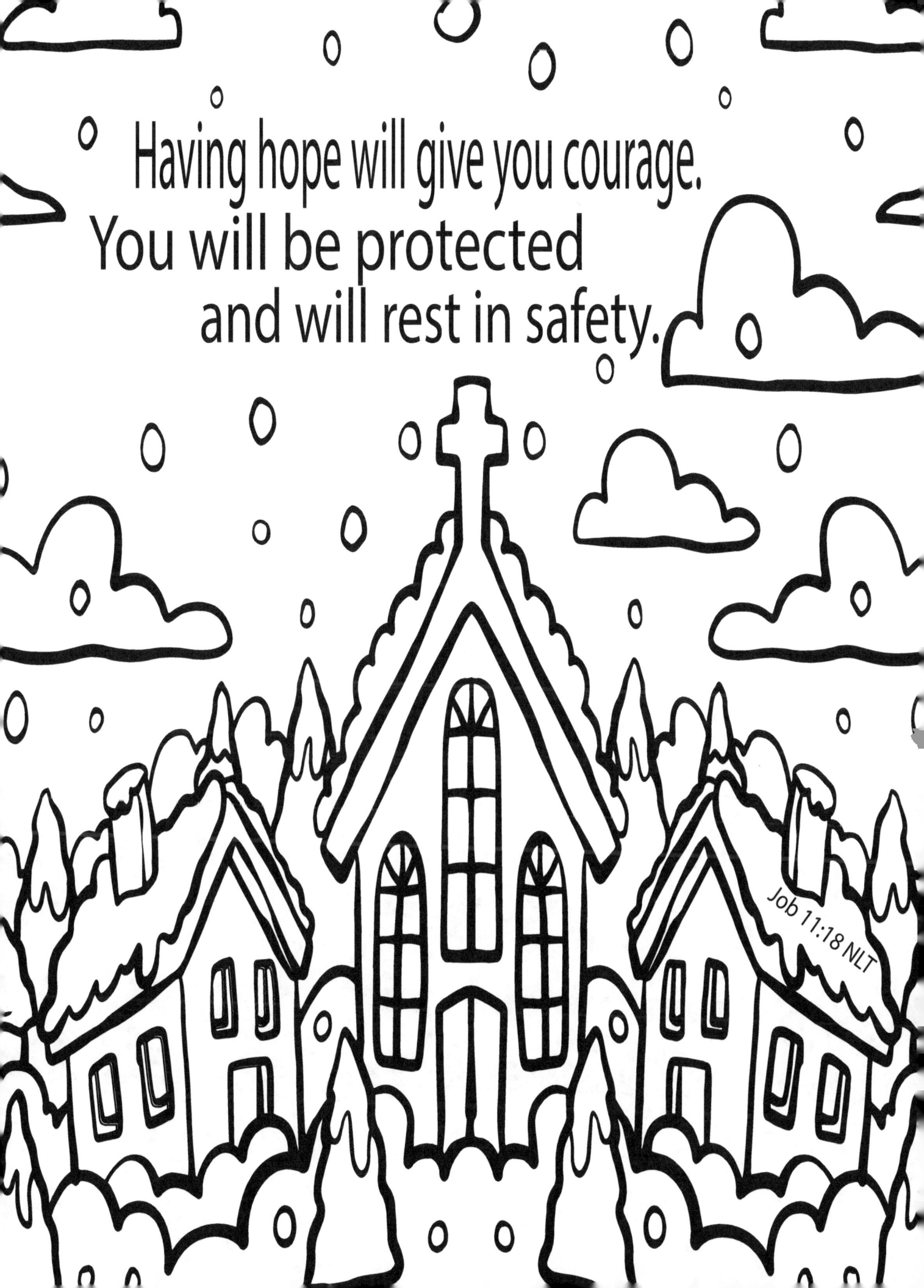

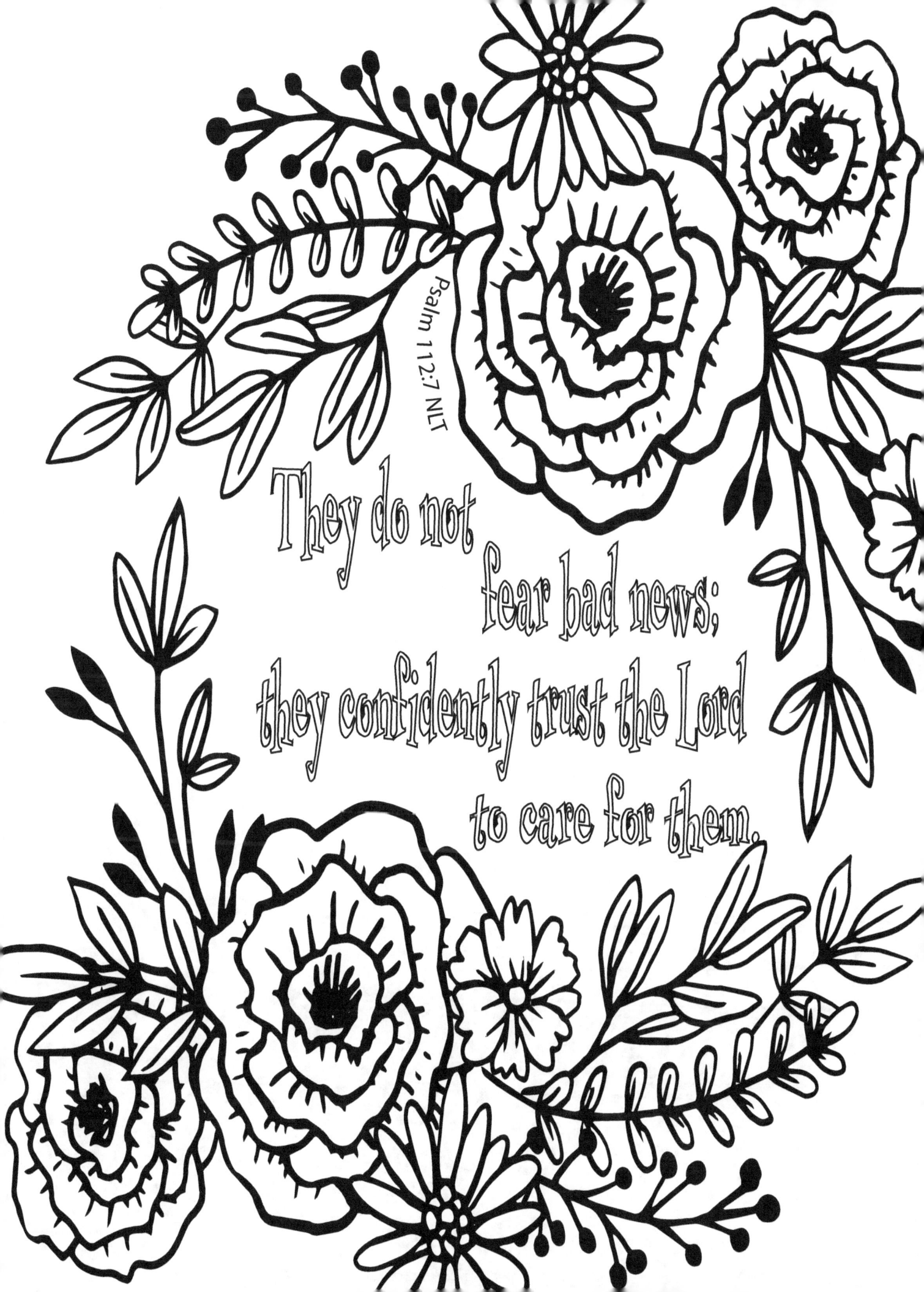

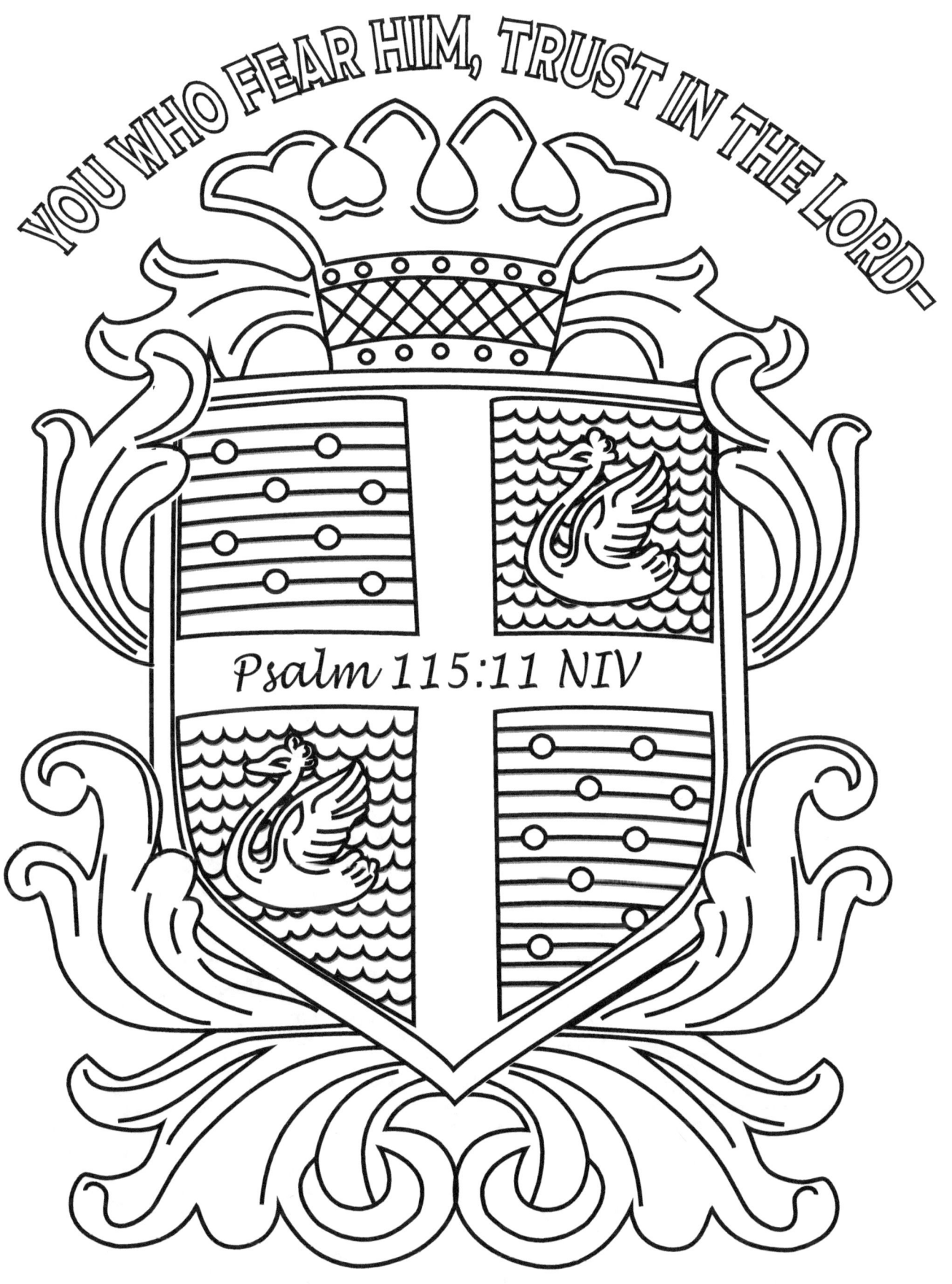

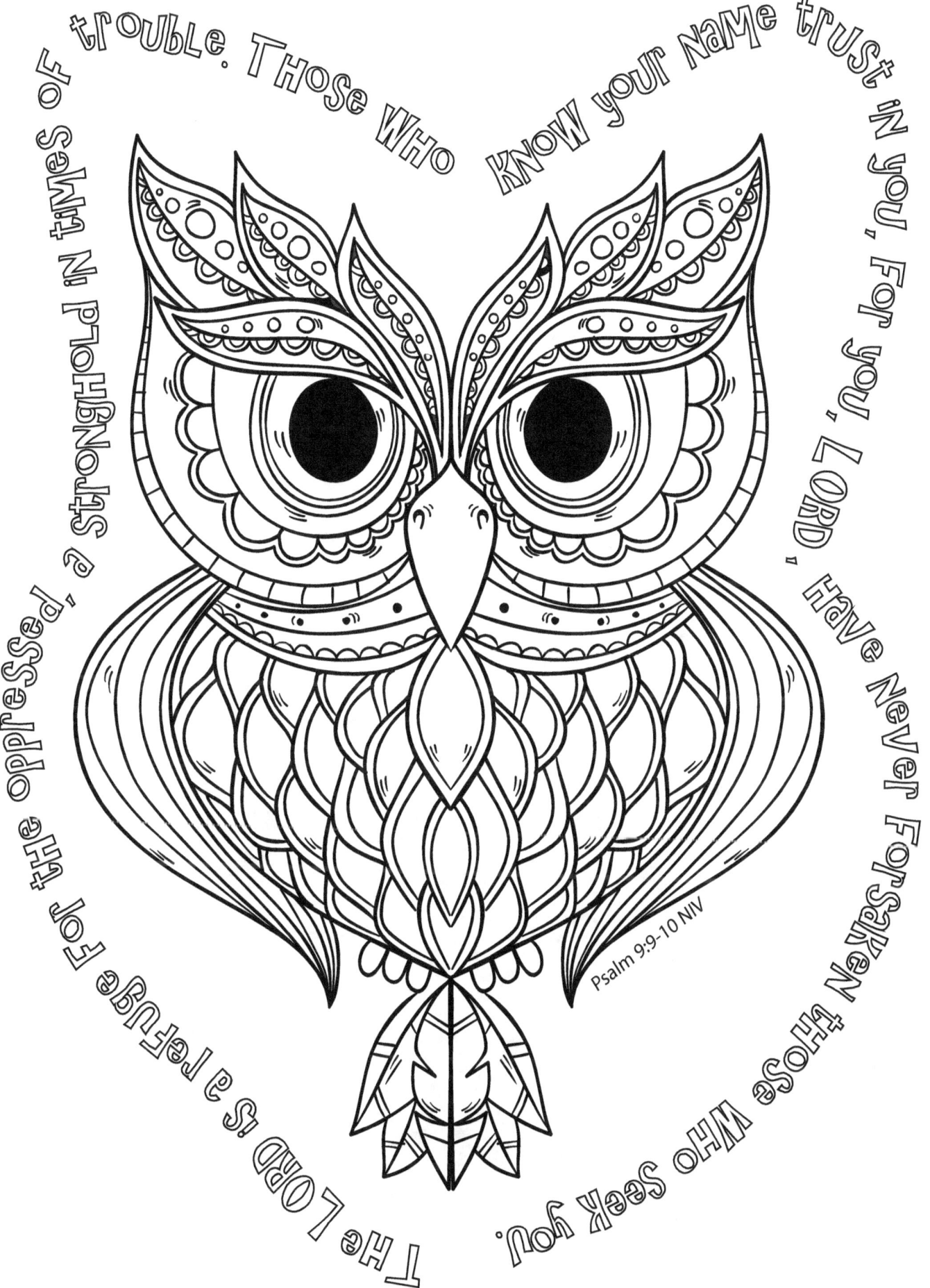

Psalm 9:9-10 NIV

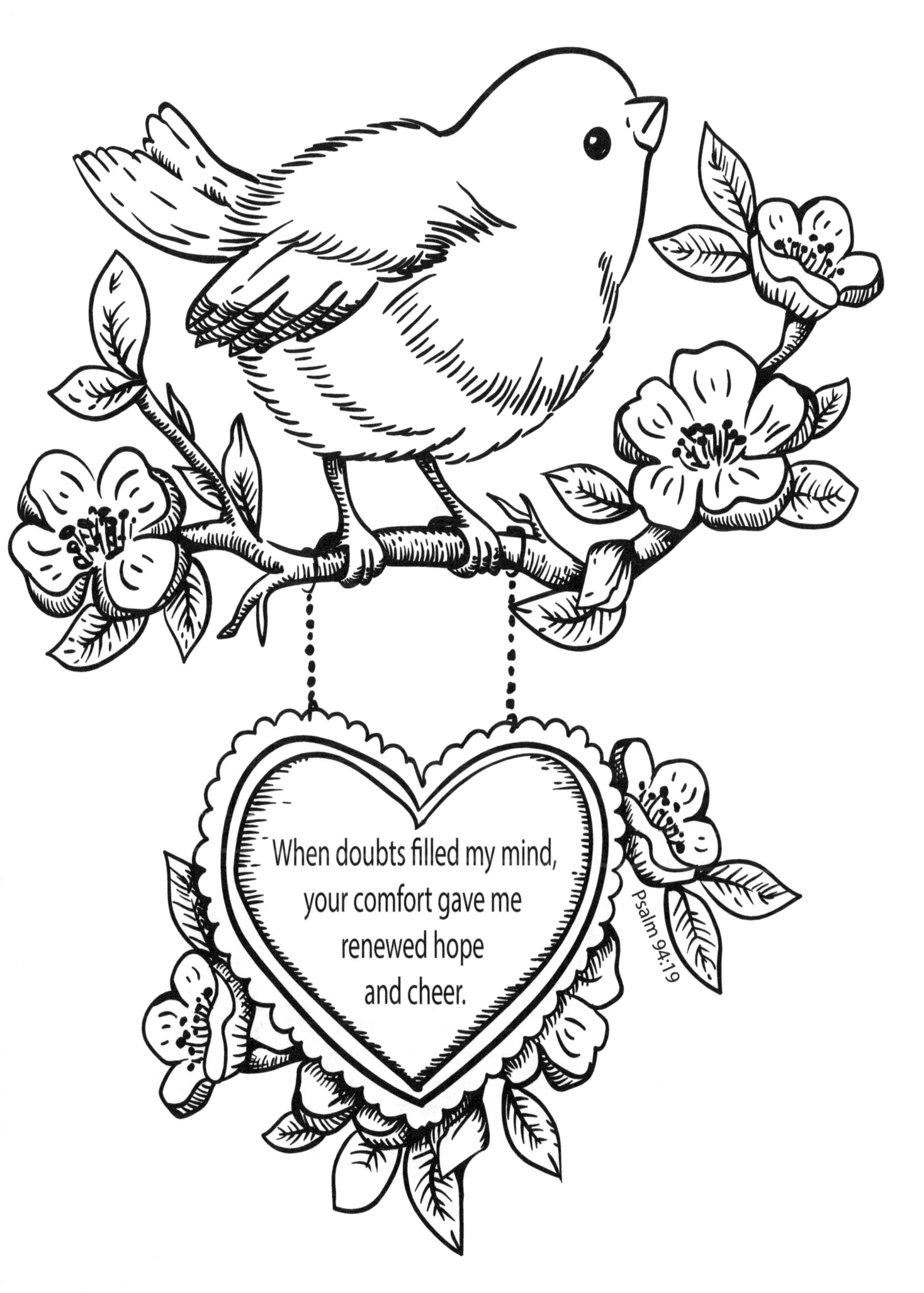

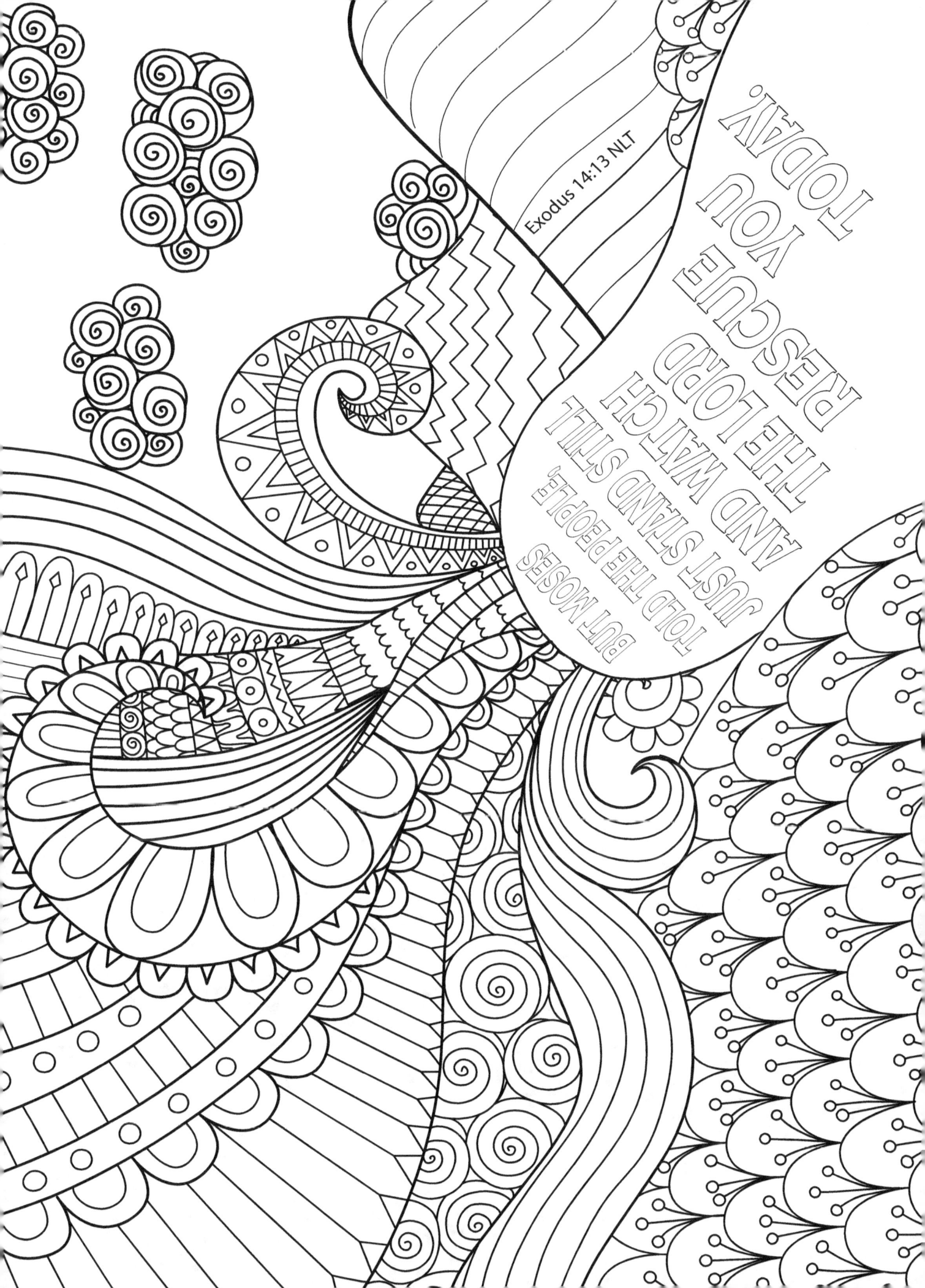

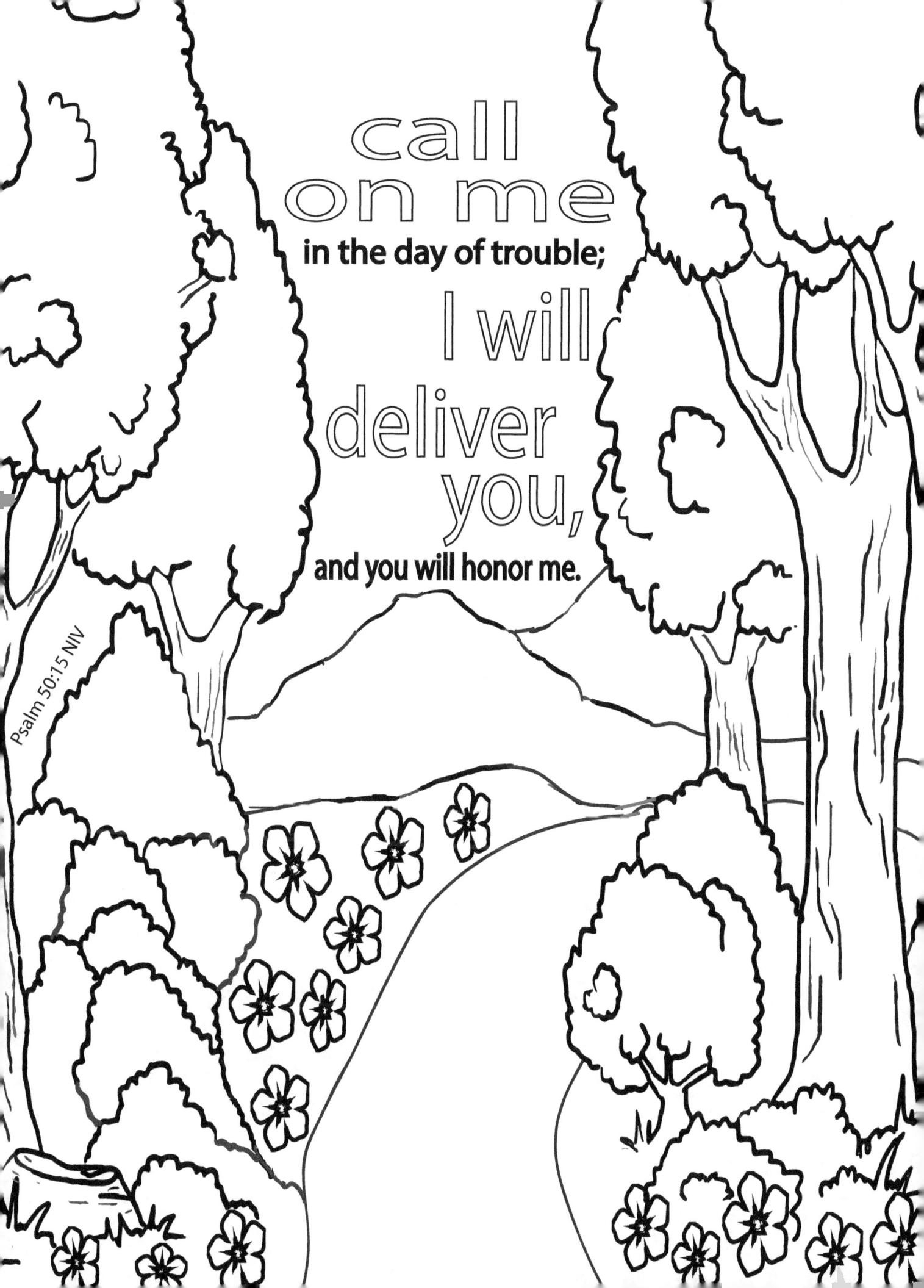

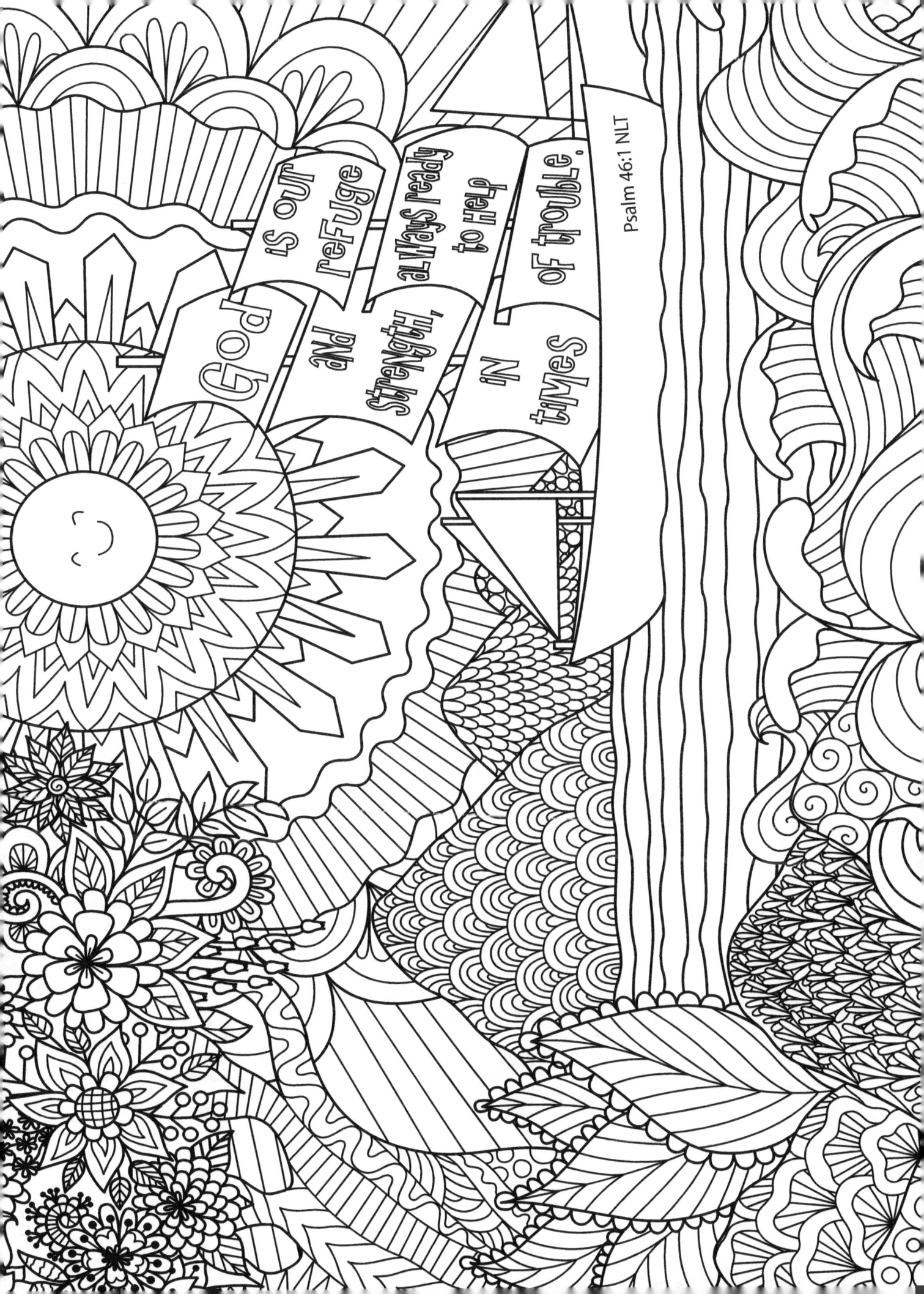

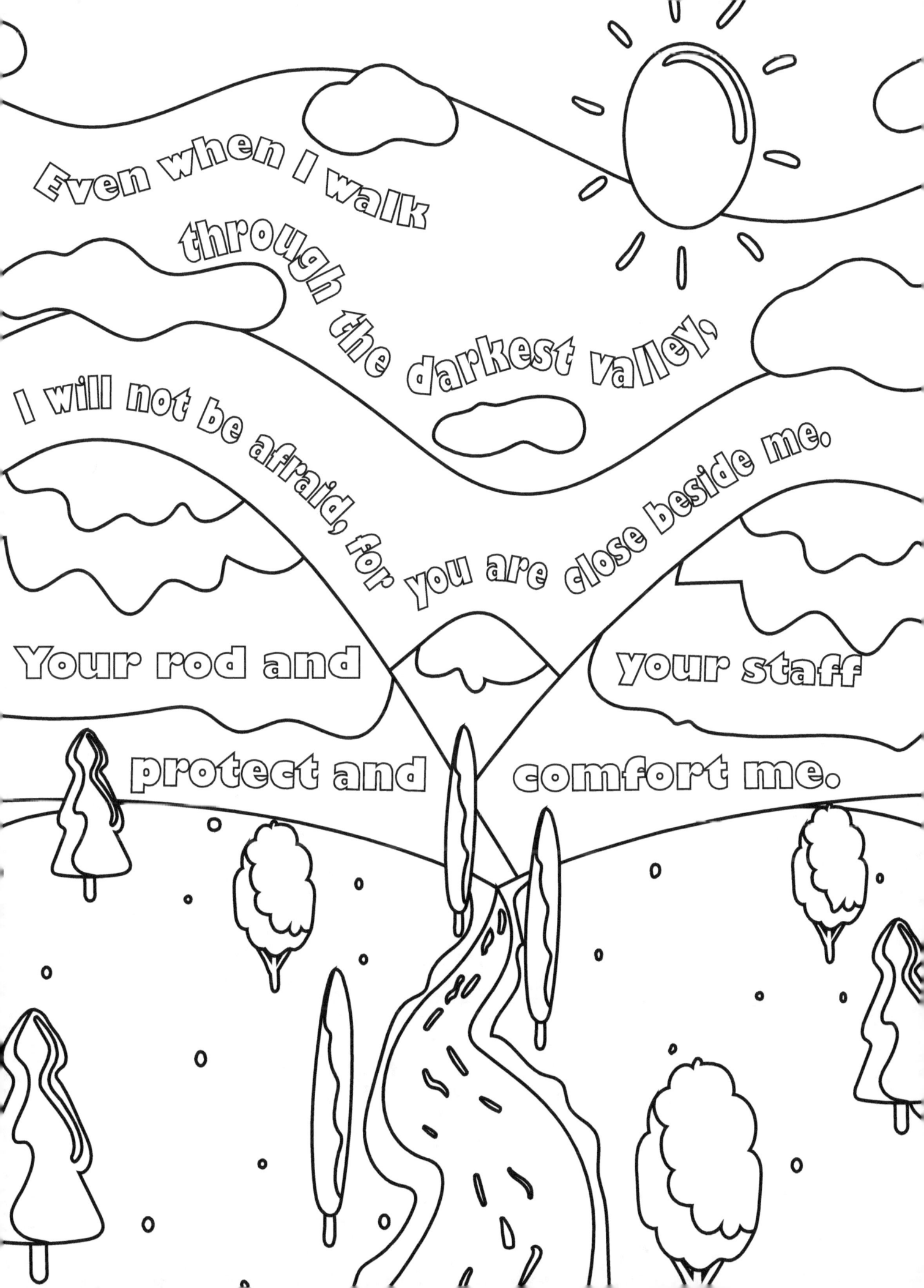

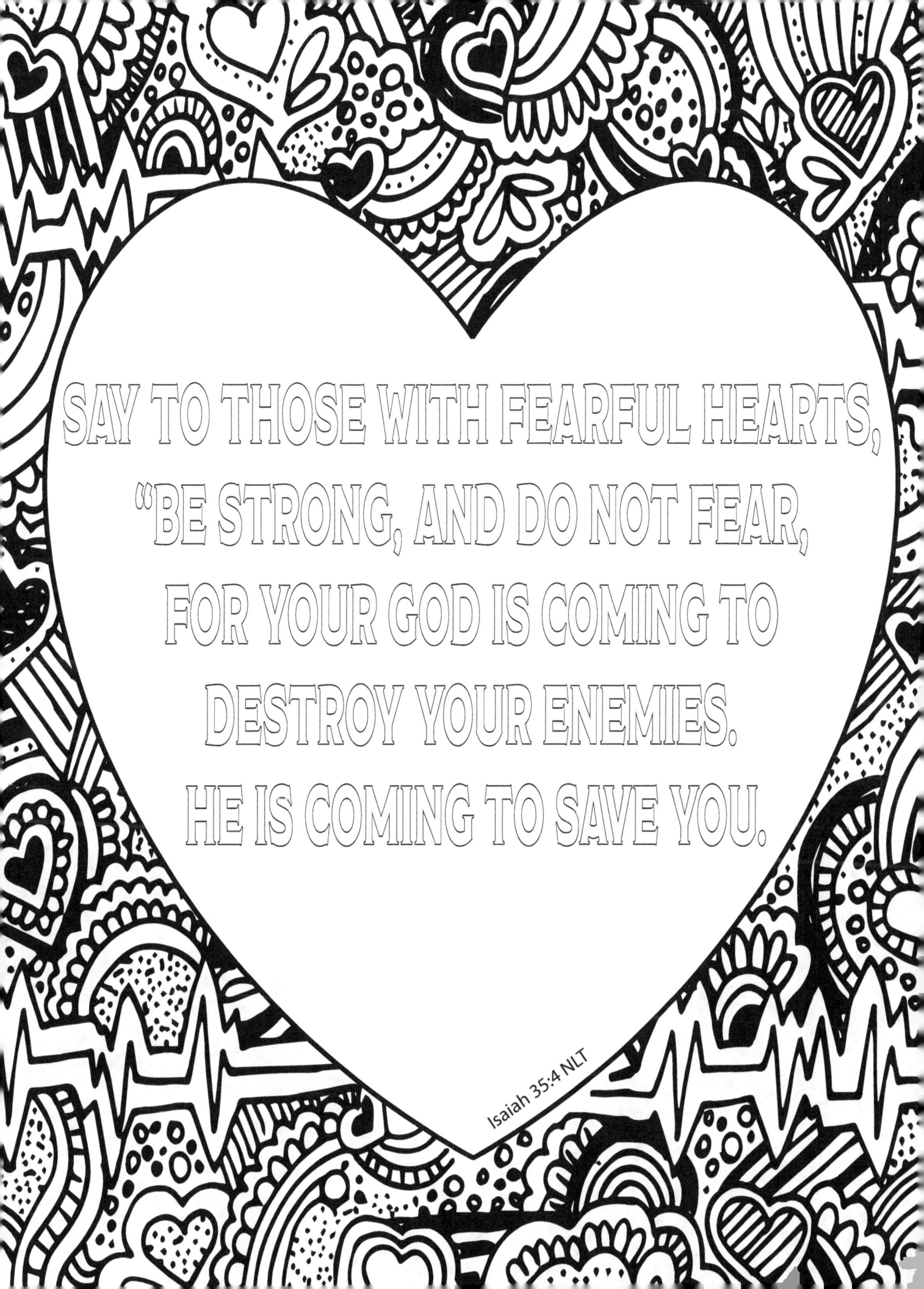

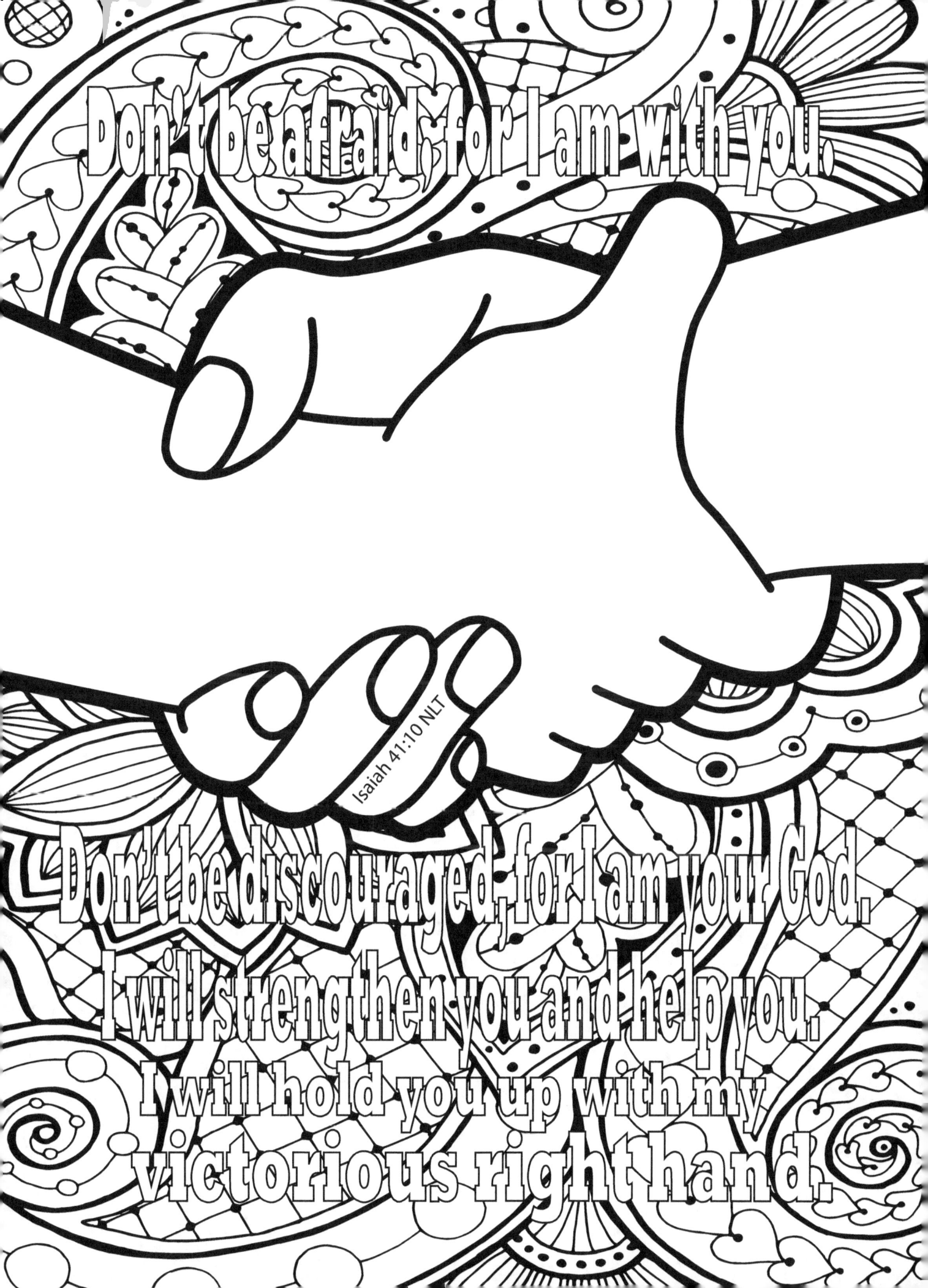

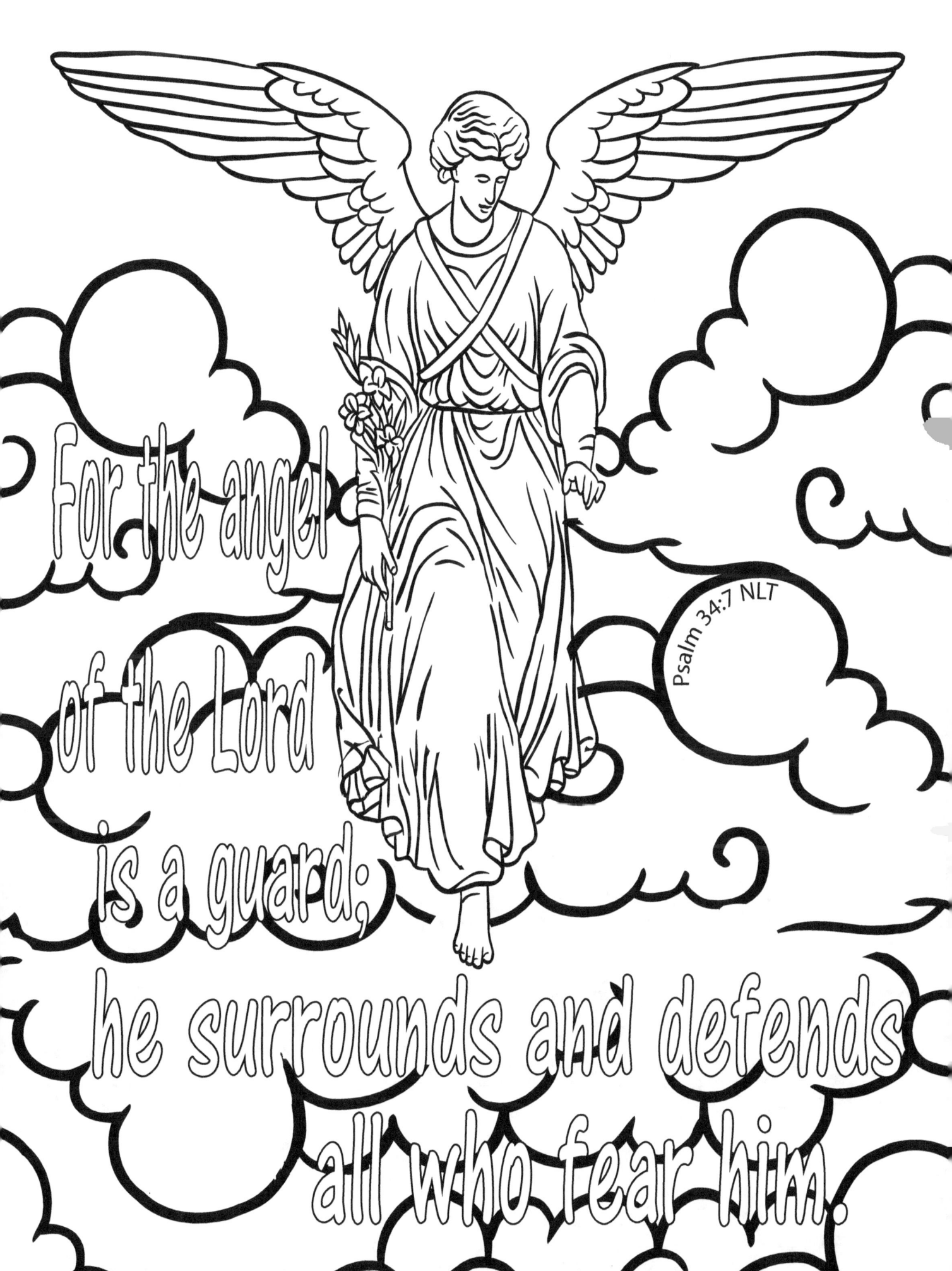

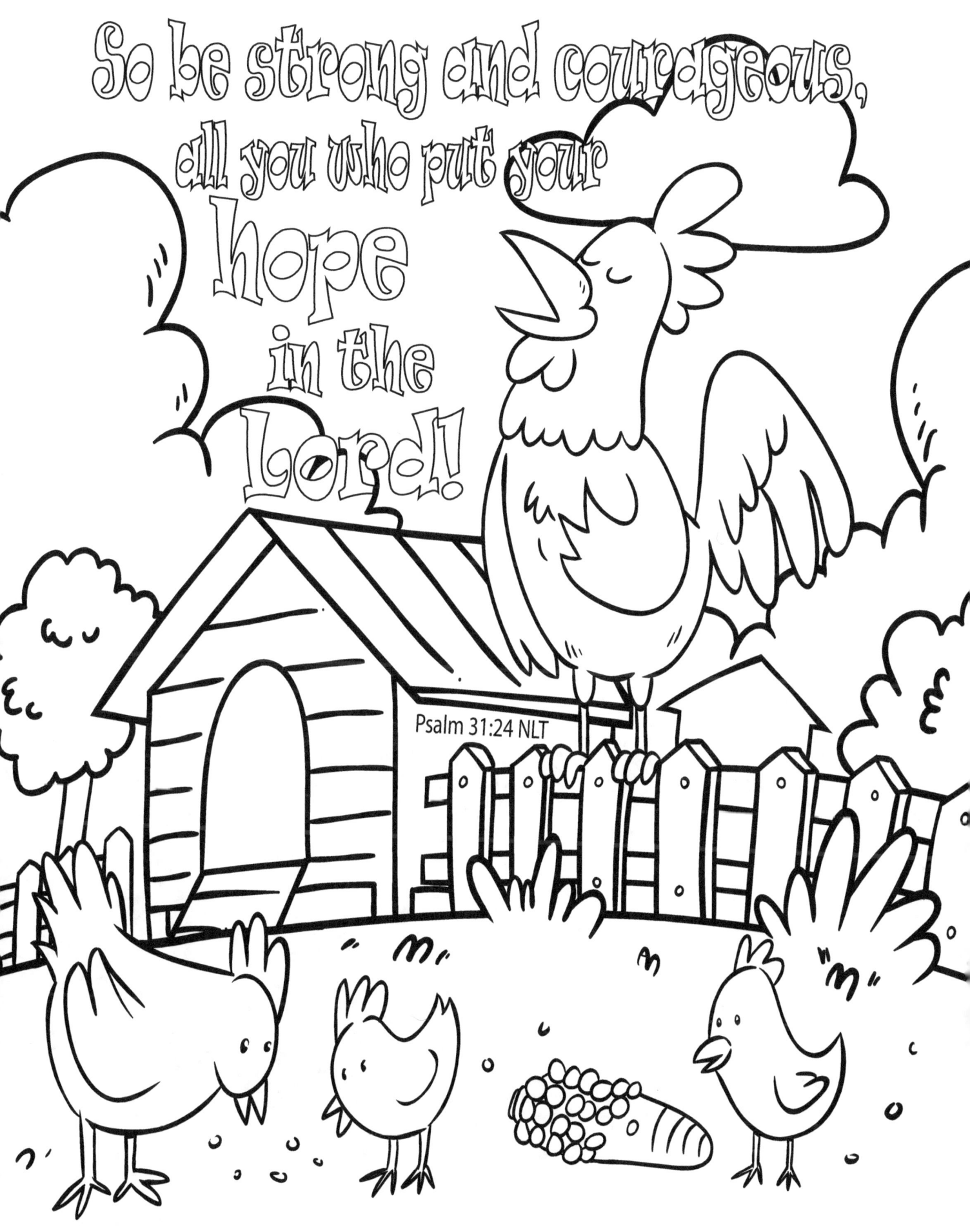

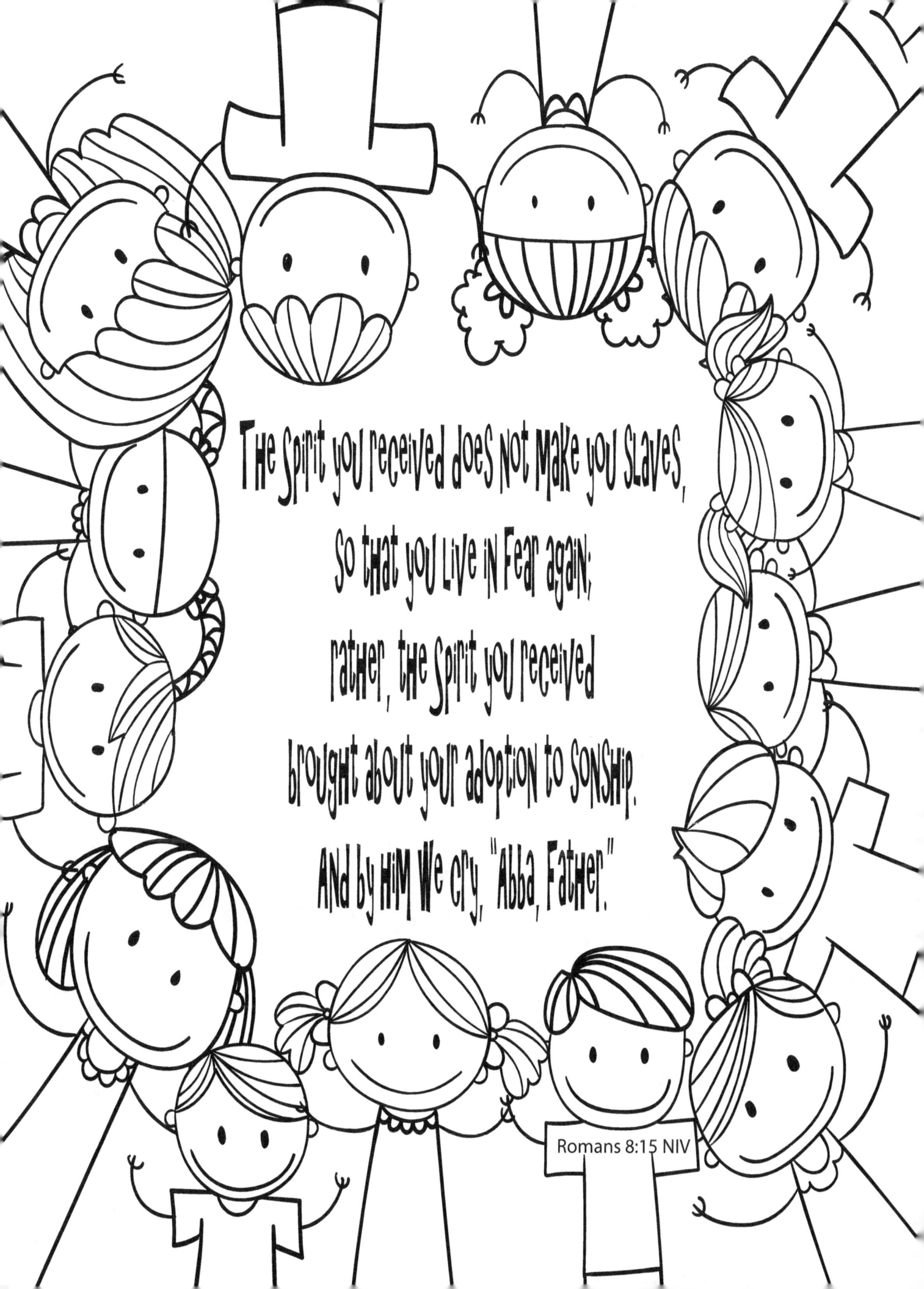

FOR I HOLD YOU BY YOUR RIGHT HAND—
I, THE LORD YOUR GOD.
AND I SAY TO YOU,
DON'T BE AFRAID. I AM HERE TO HELP YOU.

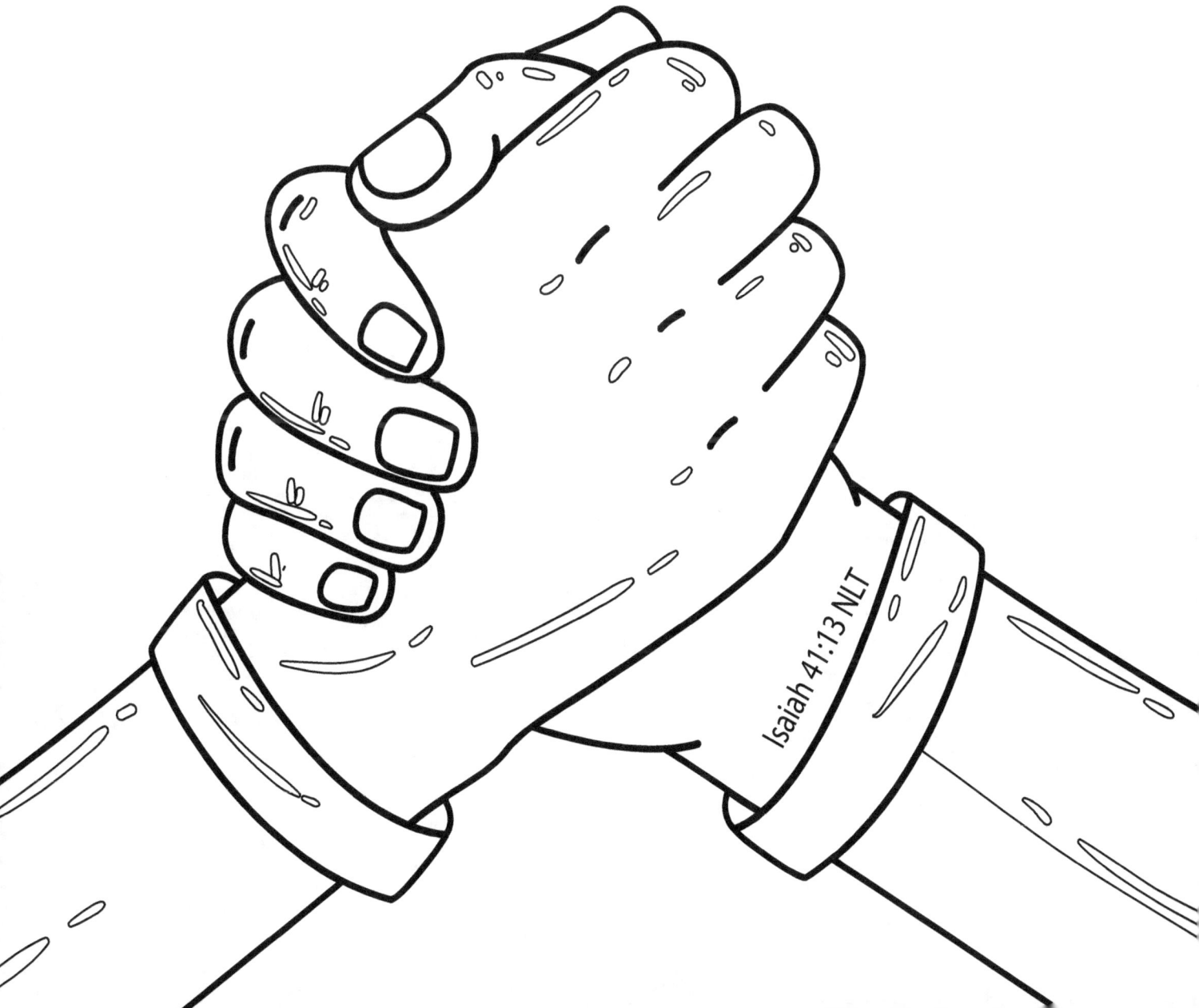

Isaiah 41:13 NLT

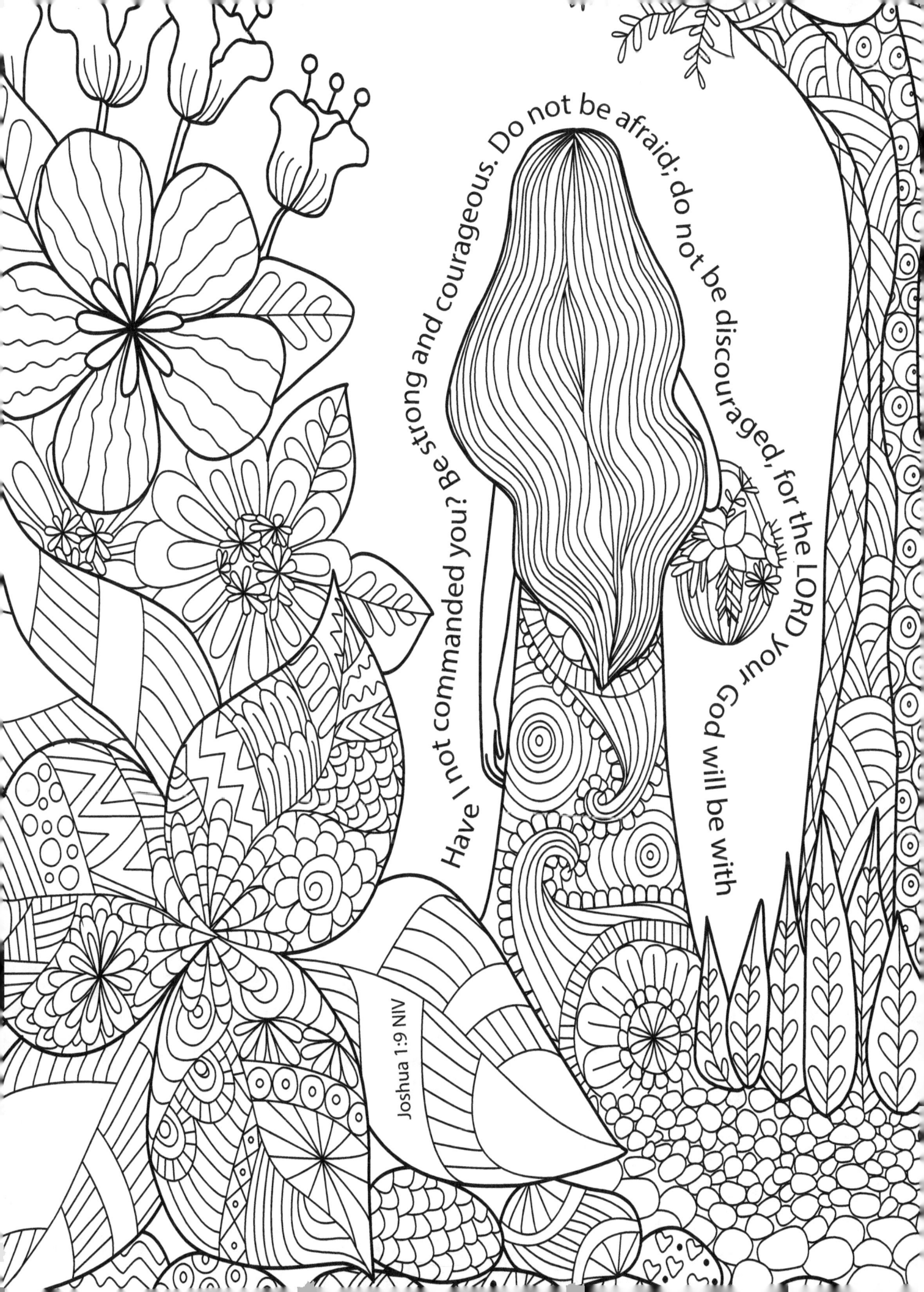

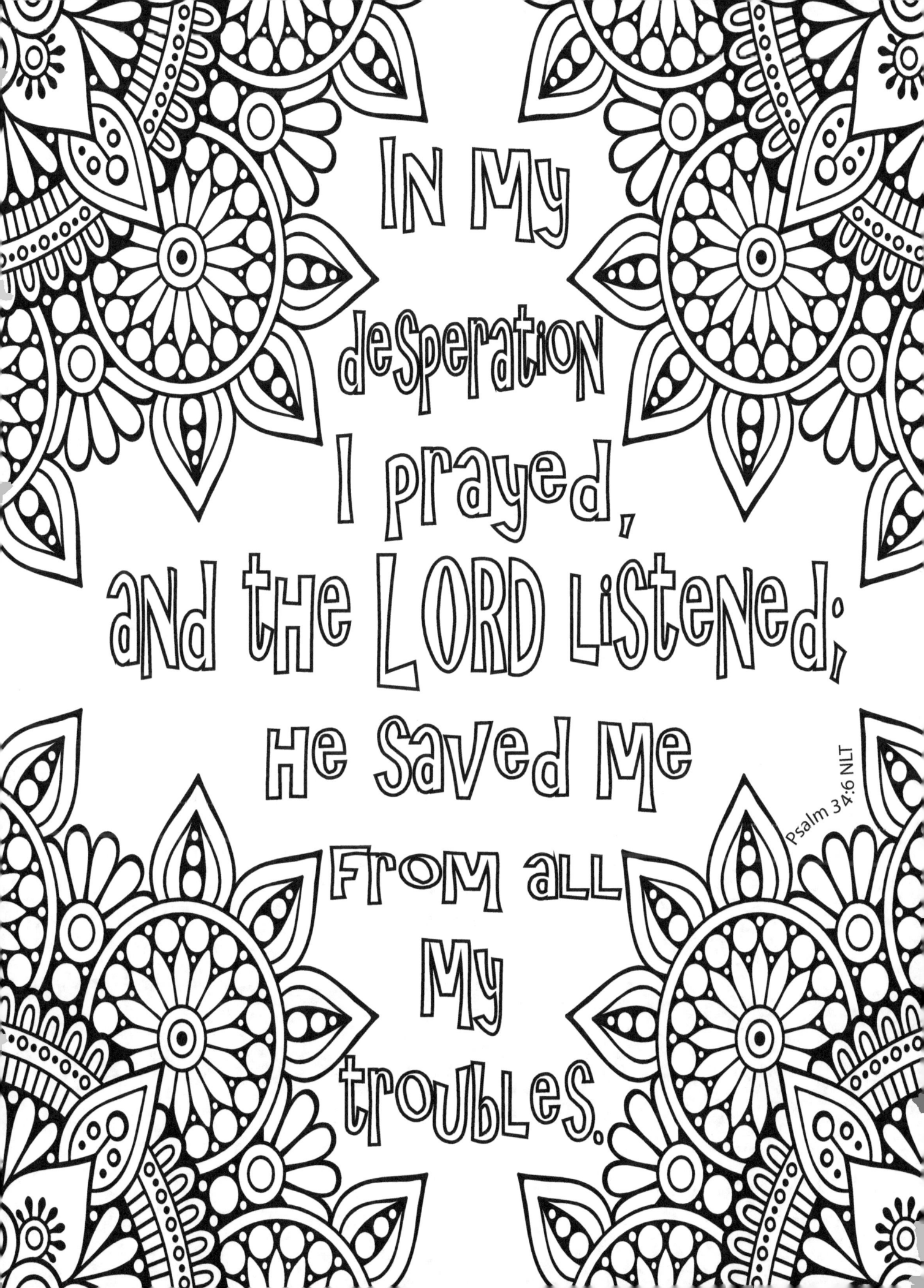

I HAVE TOLD YOU THESE THINGS, SO THAT IN ME YOU MAY HAVE **PEACE.** IN THIS WORLD YOU WILL HAVE TROUBLE. BUT TAKE HEART! I HAVE OVERCOME THE WORLD.

John 16:33 NIV

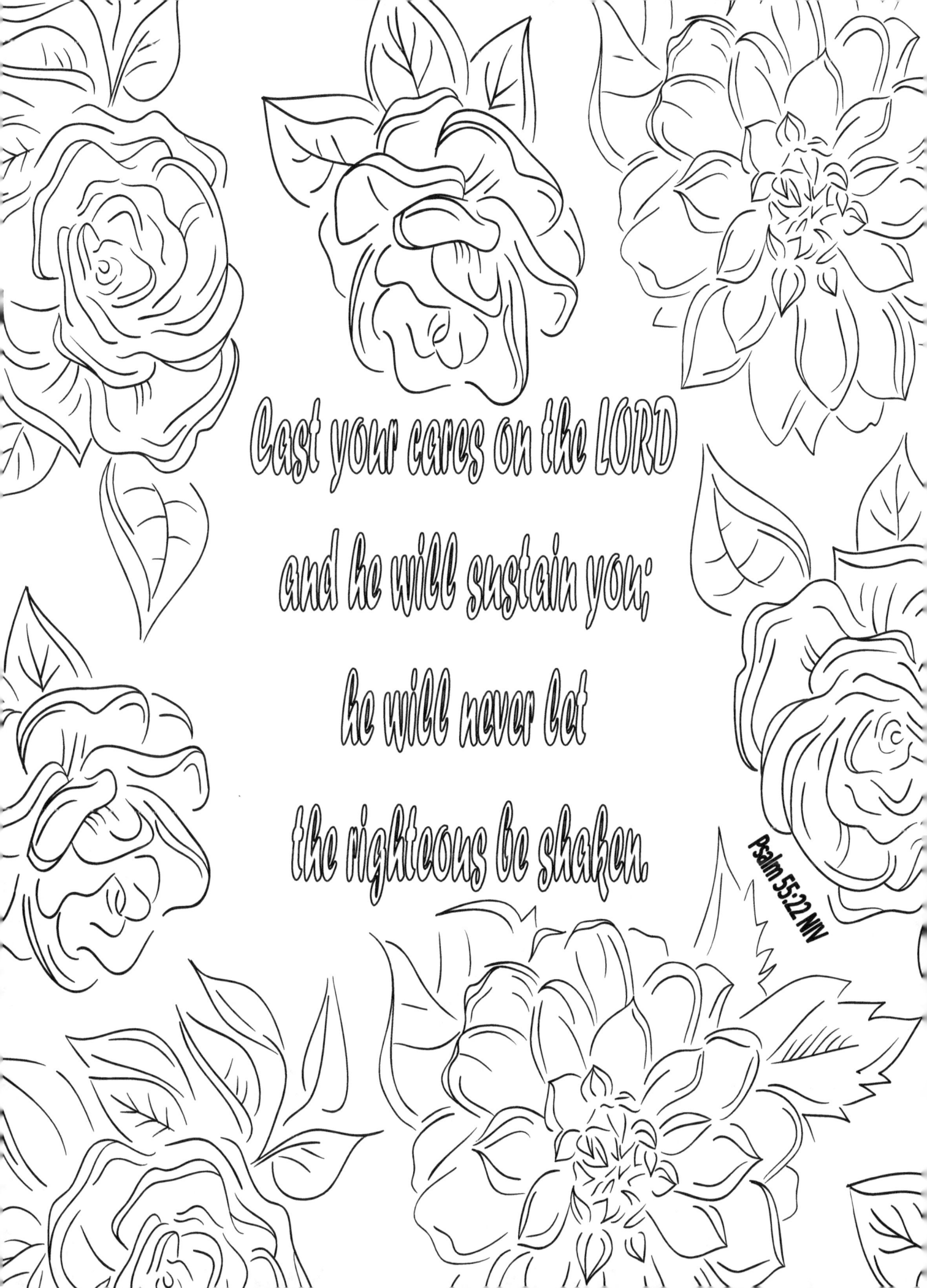

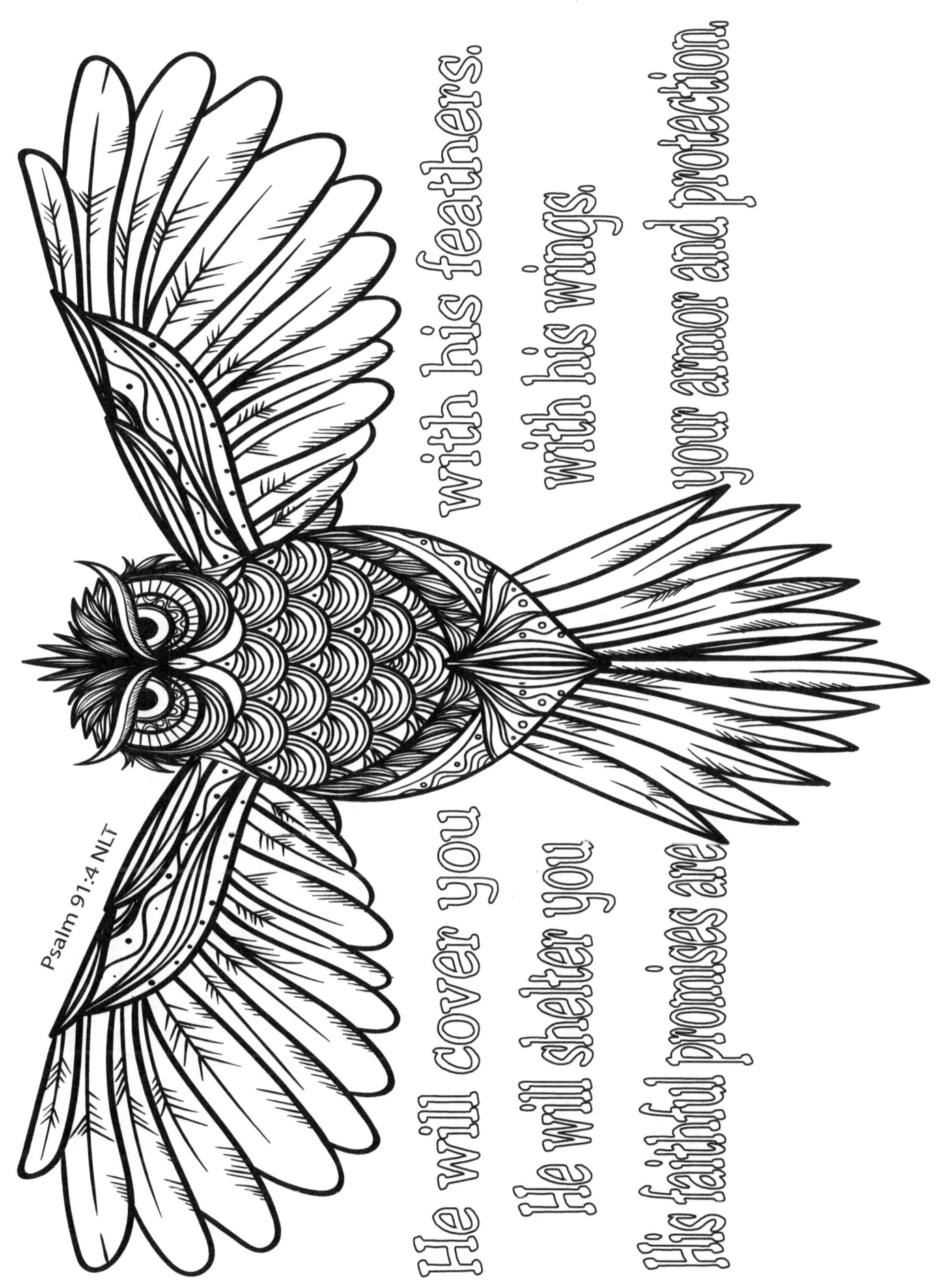

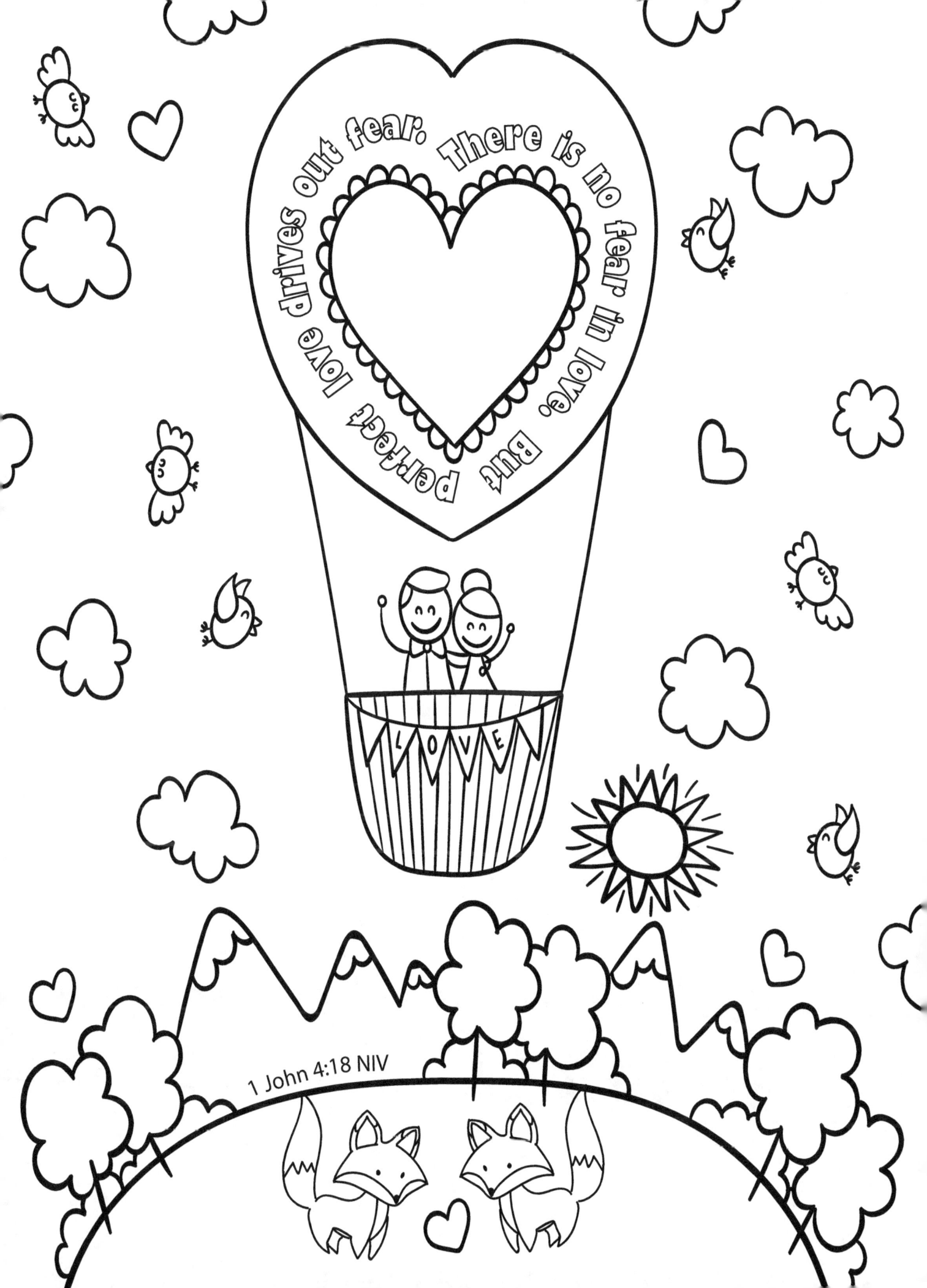

1 John 4:18 NIV

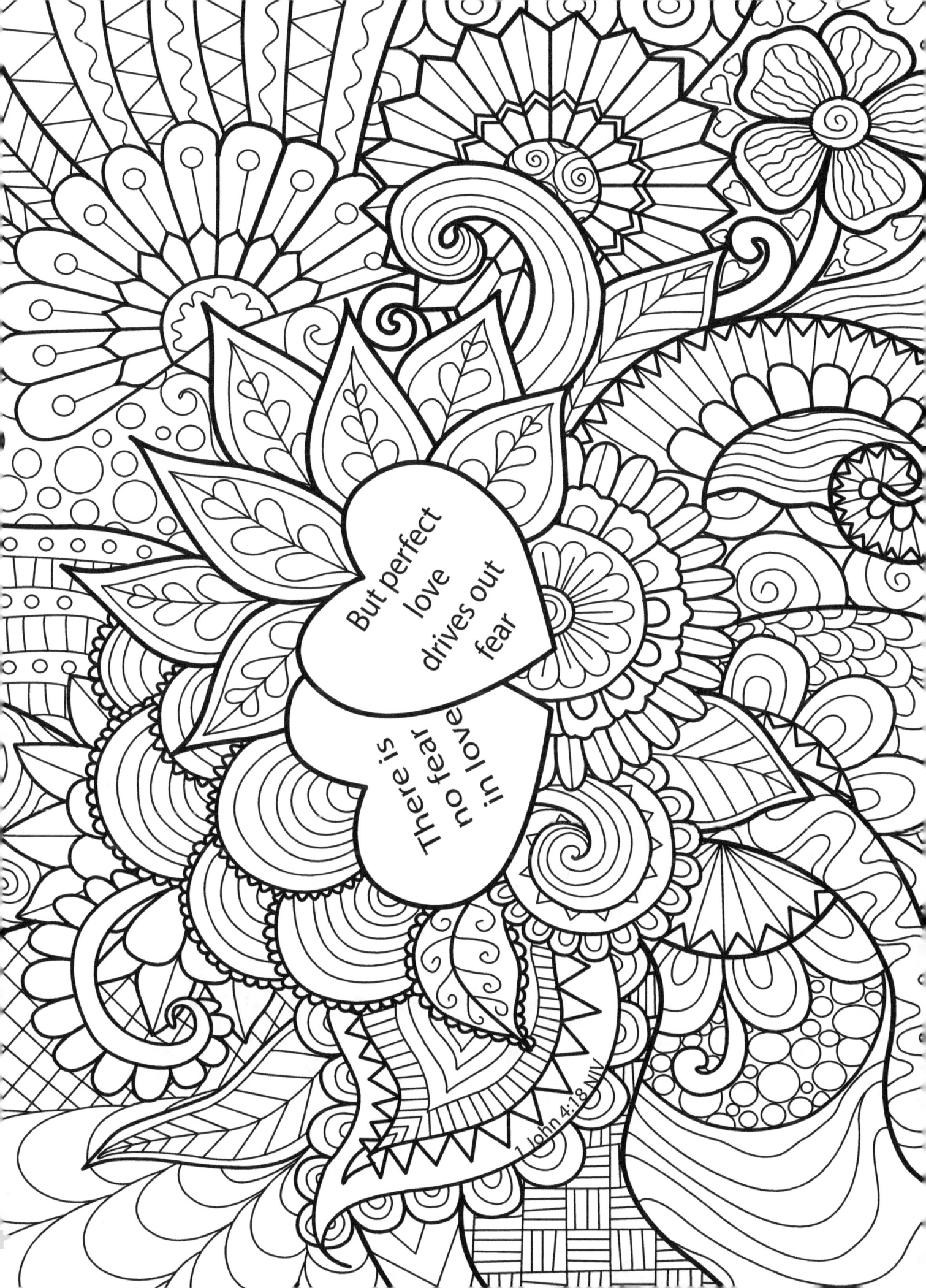

When I am afraid,
I put my trust in you.
In God, whose word I praise—
in God I trust
and am not afraid.
What can mere mortals
do to me?

Psalm 56:3-4 NIV

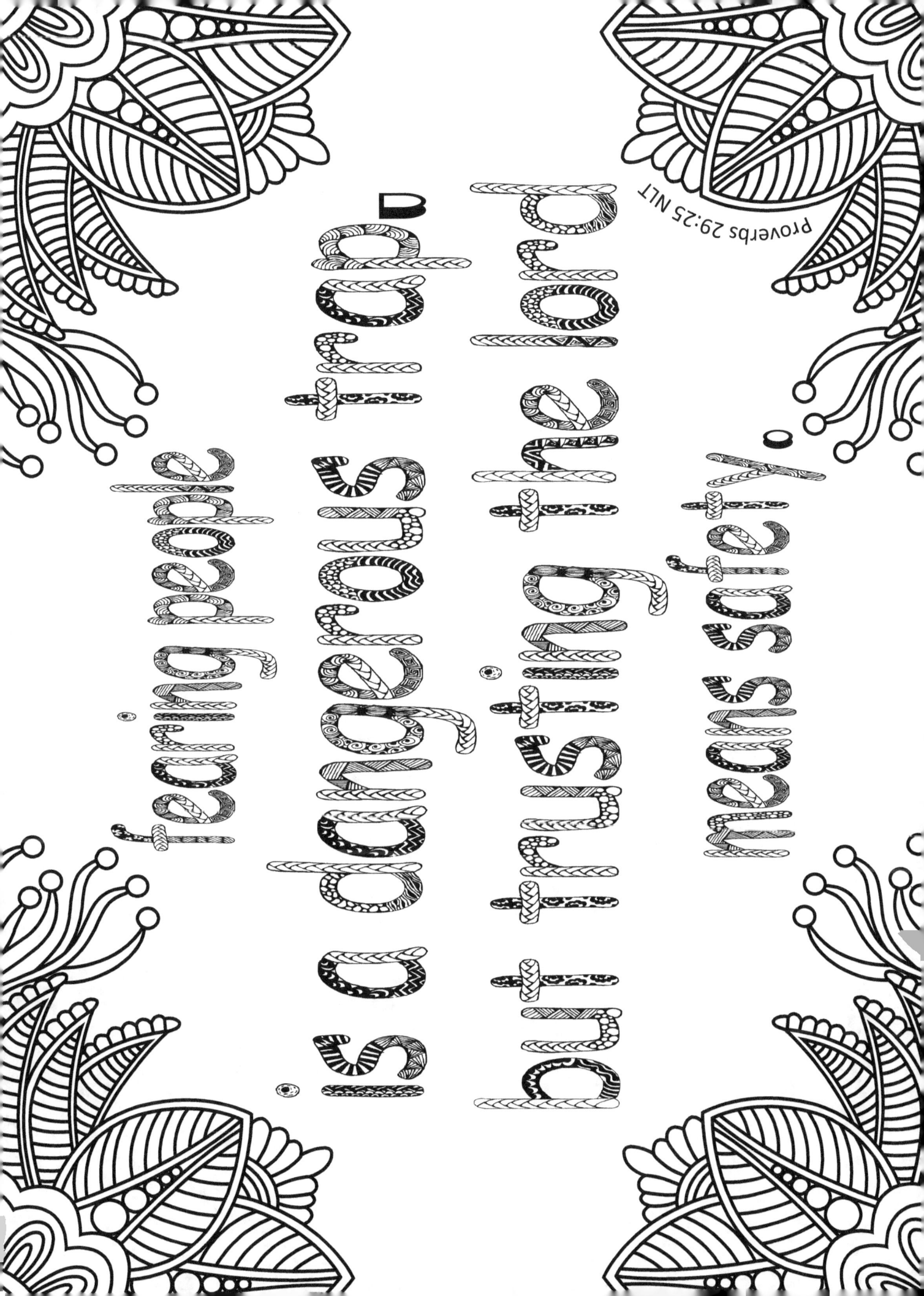

Fearing people is a dangerous trap, but trusting the Lord means safety.

Proverbs 29:25 NLT

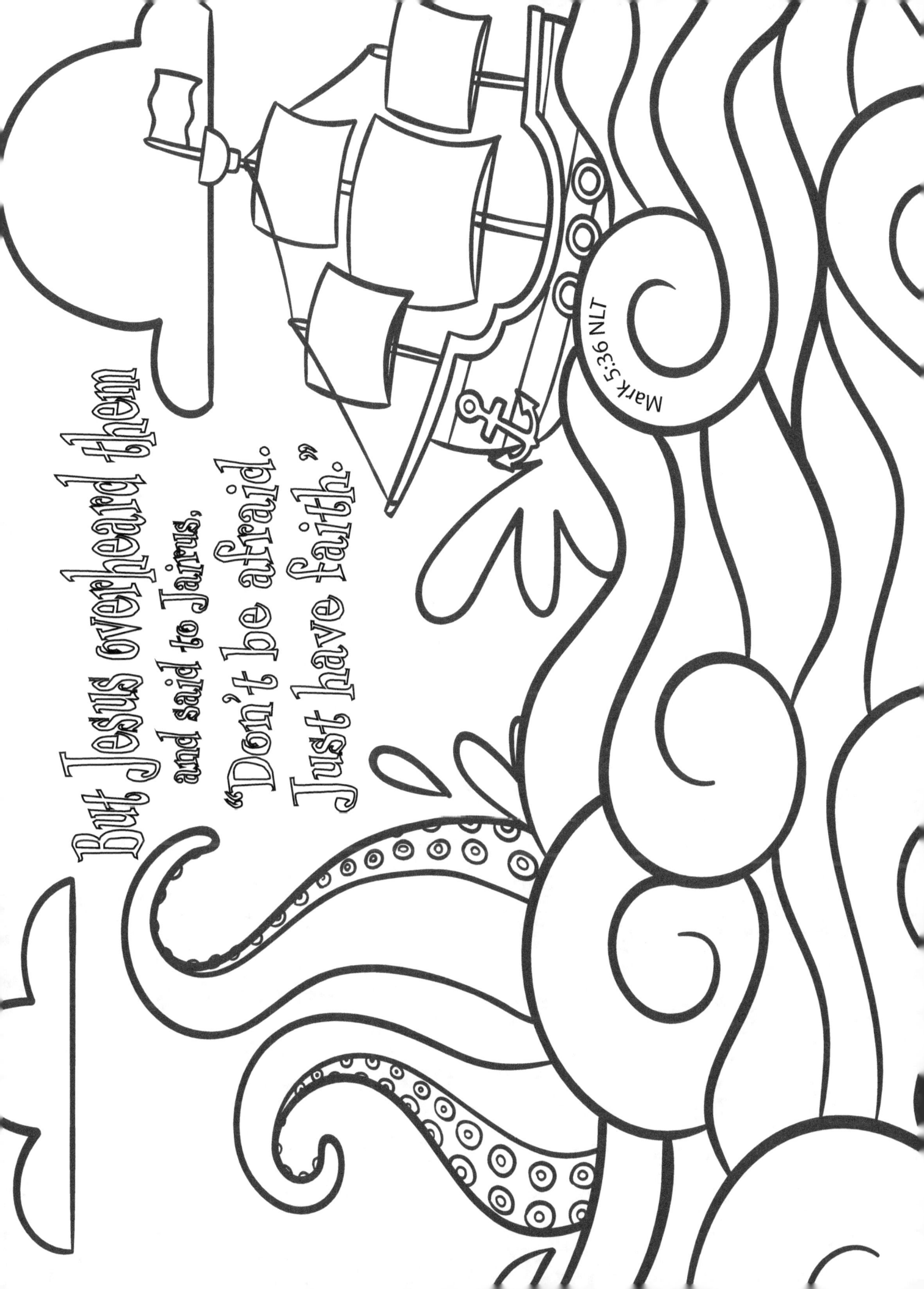

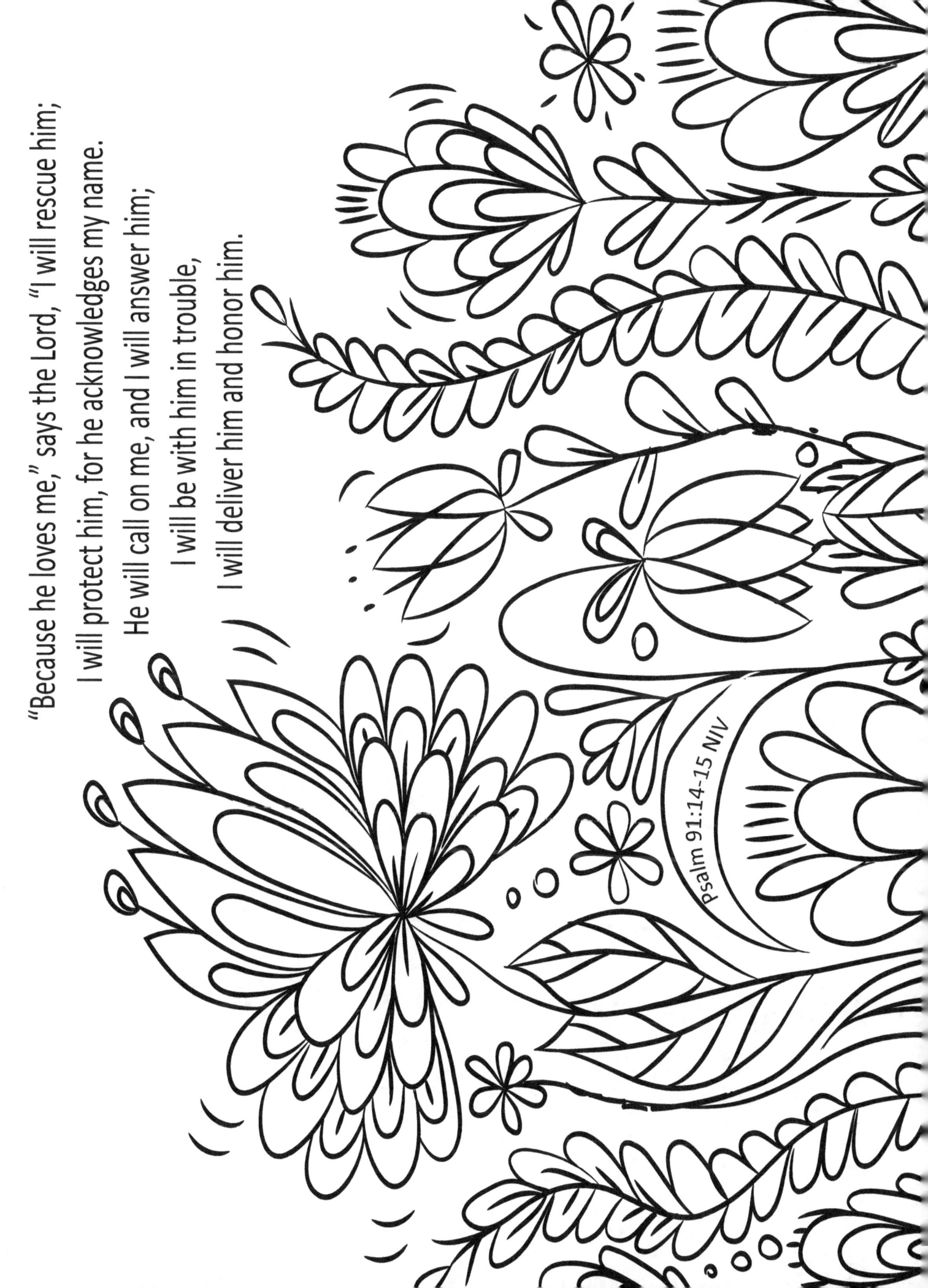

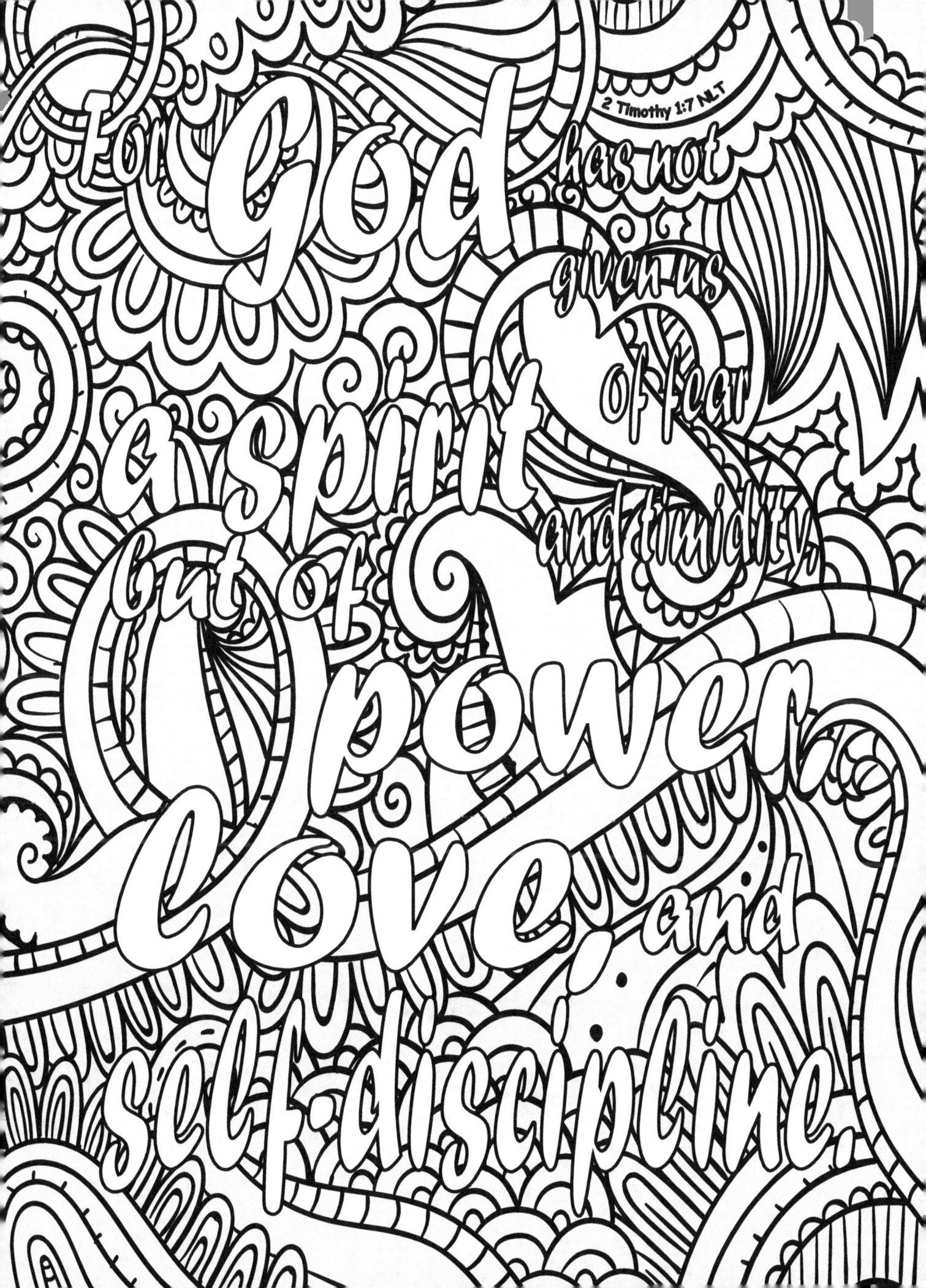

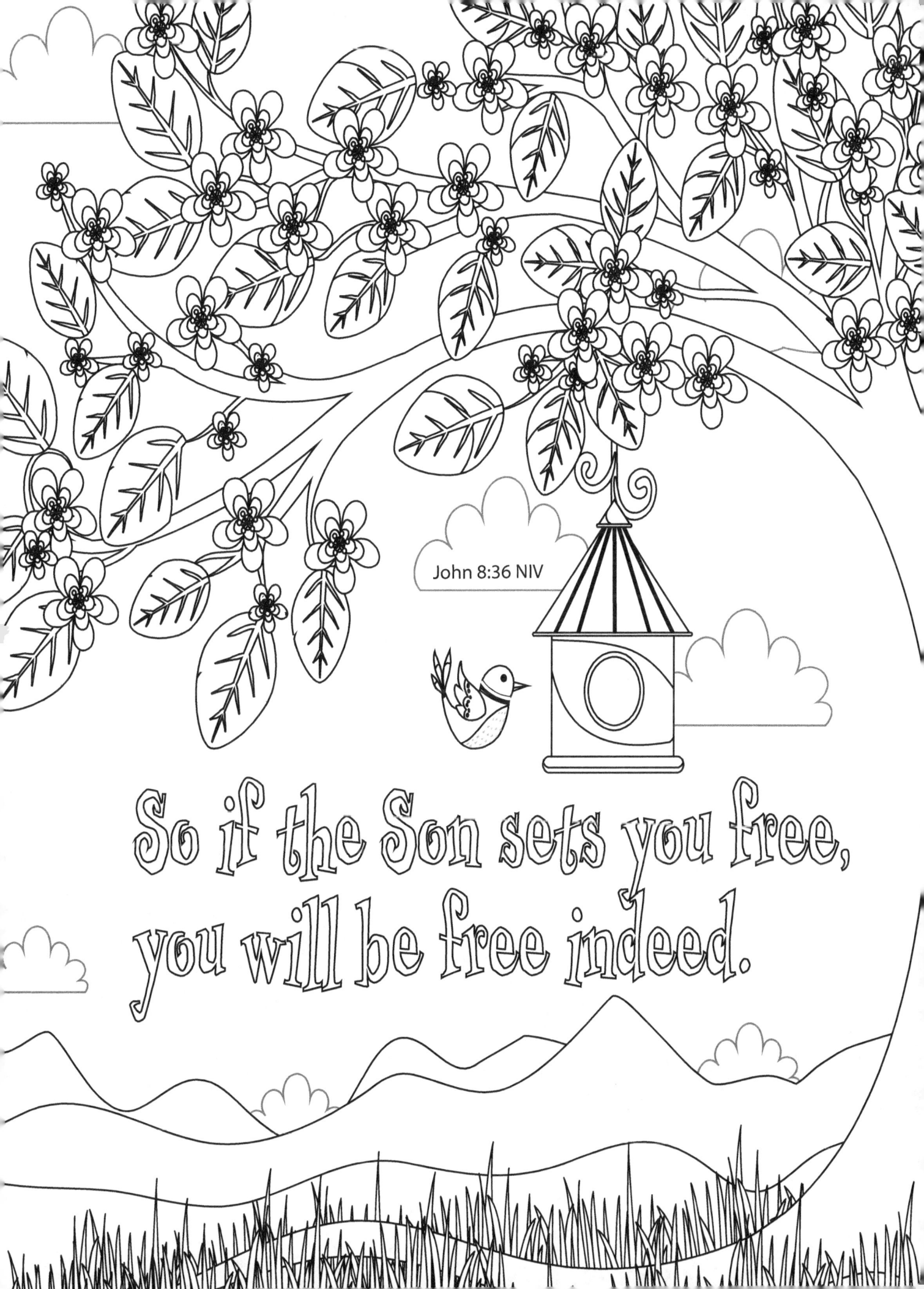

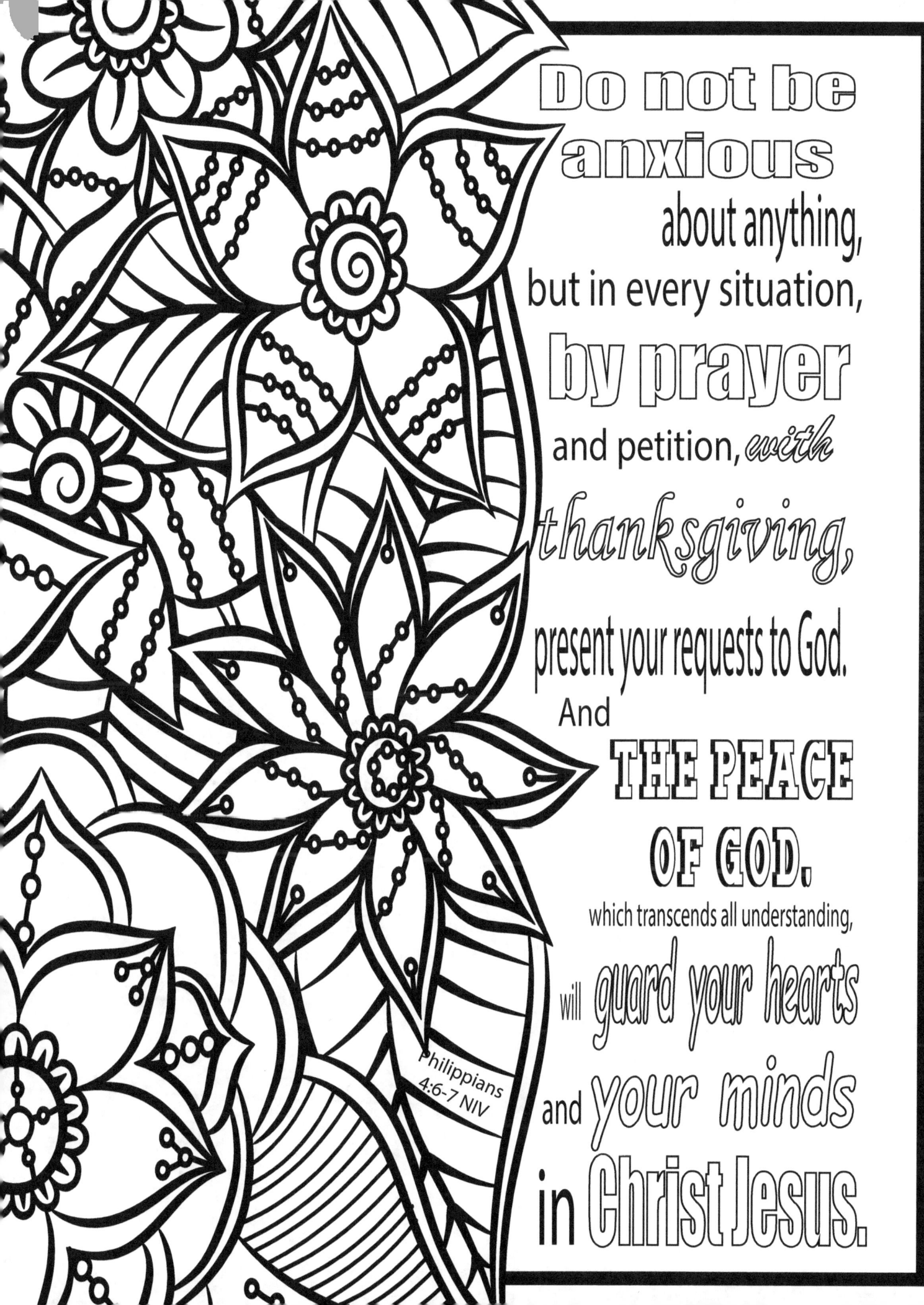

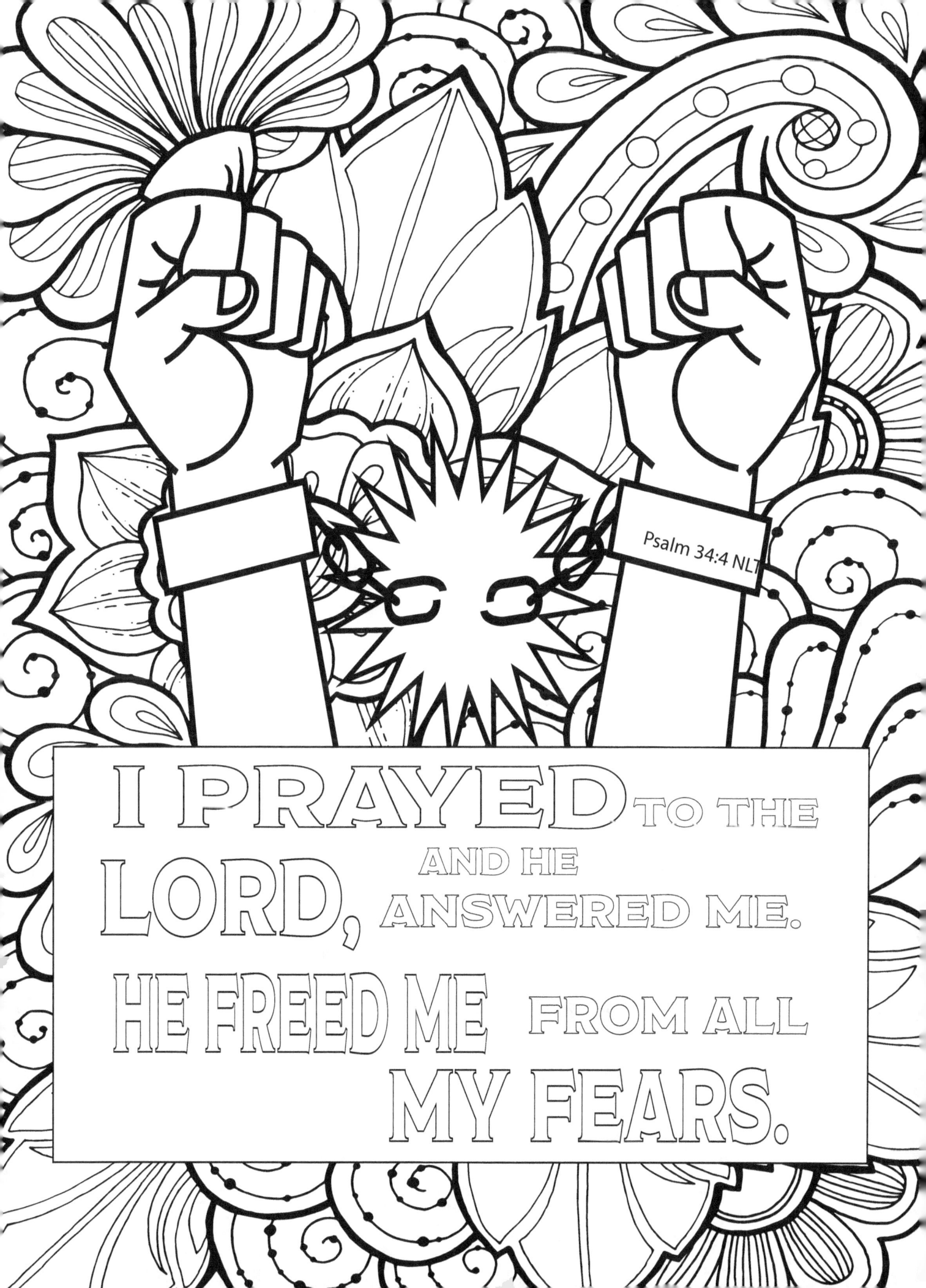

He gives strength
to the weary
and increases the power
of the weak.

Isaiah 40:29 NIV

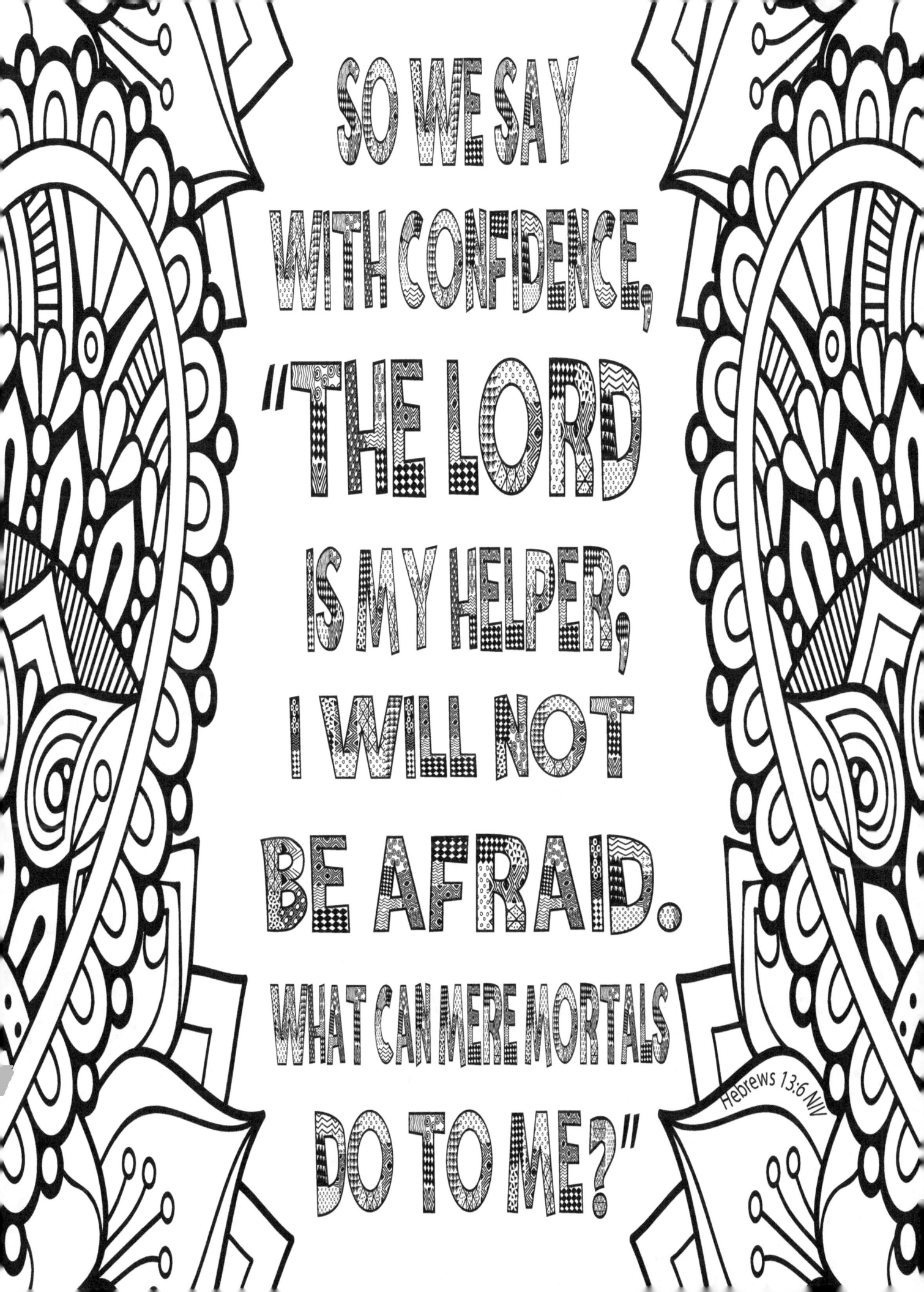

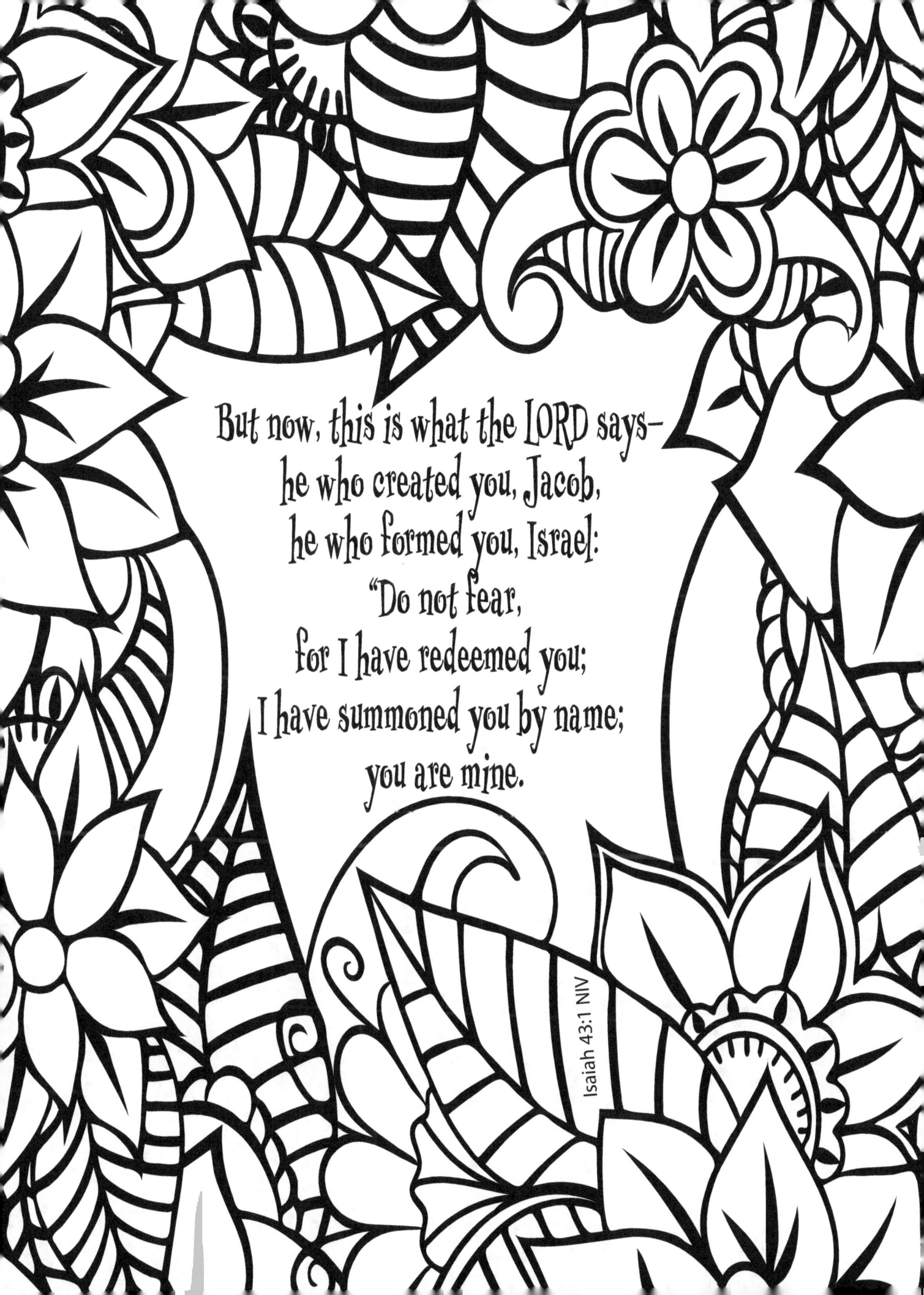

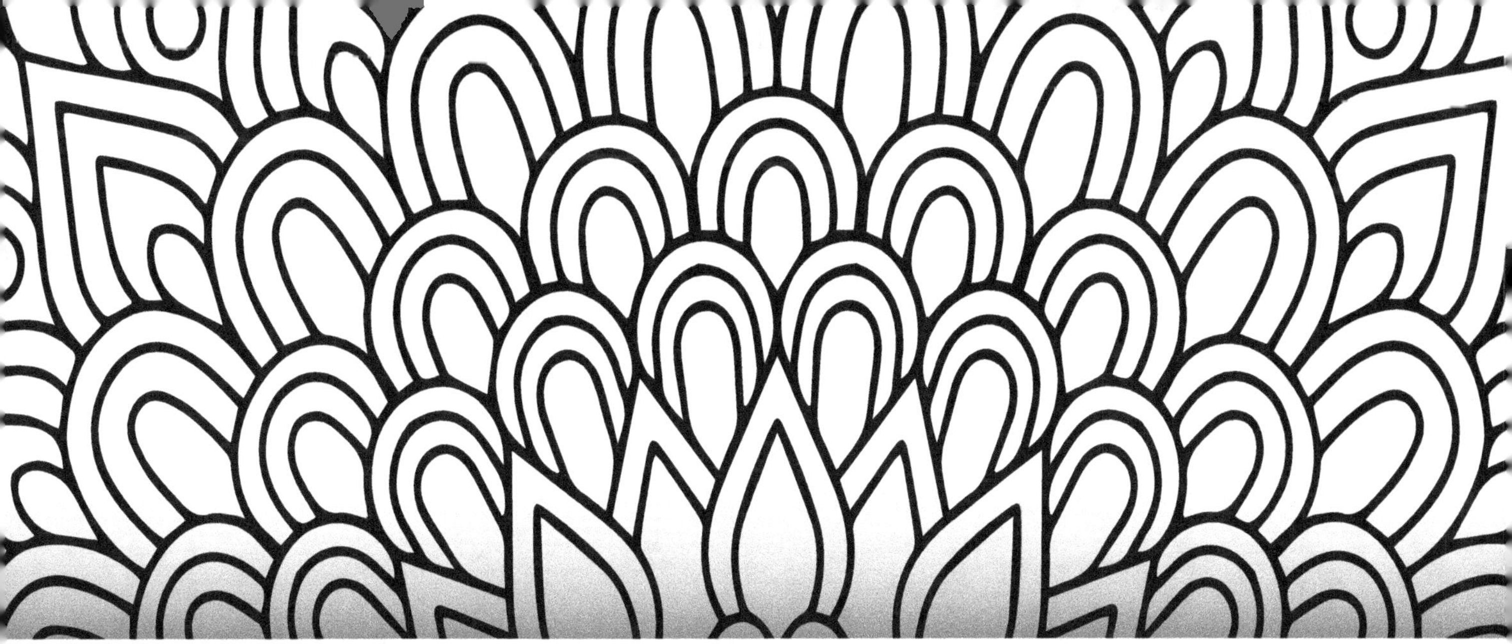

Deuteronomy 31:6 NIV

Be strong and courageous. Do not be afraid or terrified because of them, for the LORD your God goes with you; he will never leave you nor forsake you."

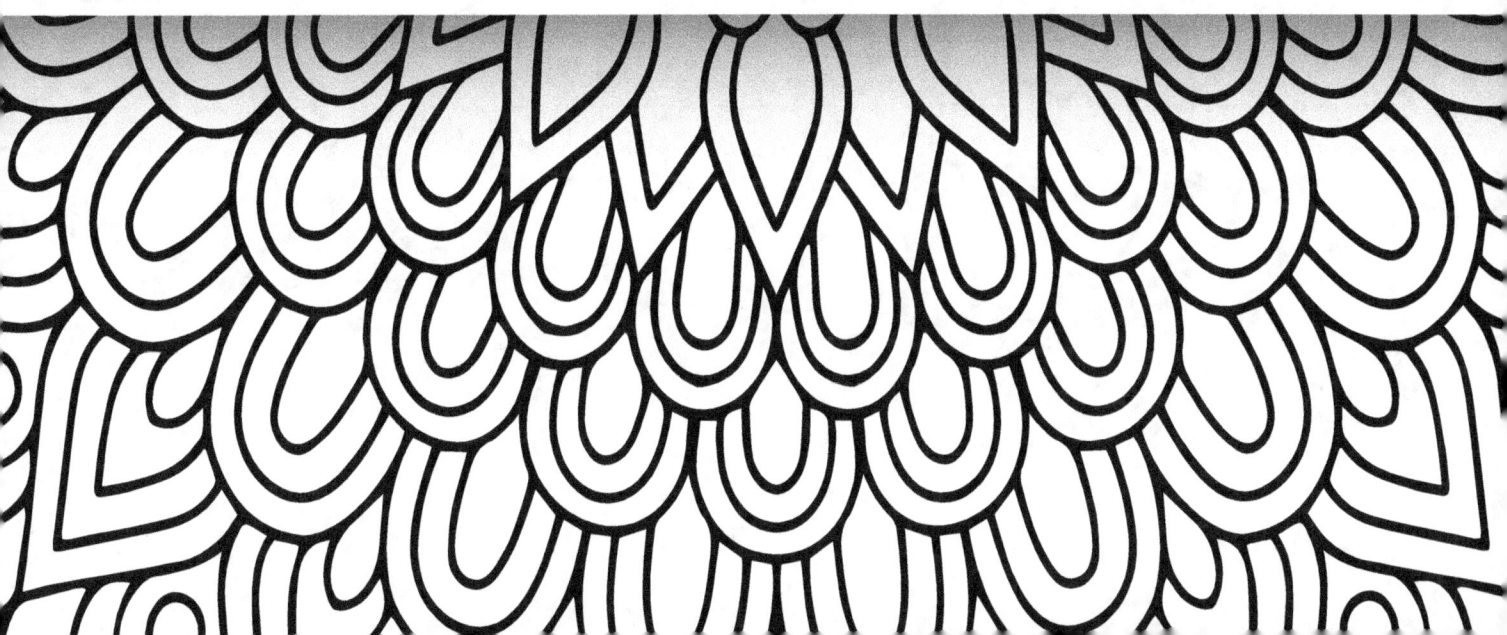

BLOTTING PAGE

Use This Page To Prevent Marker Bleed Through. Or To Test And Keep Track Of Your Color Selections So You Can Pick Just The Right Colors Or Not Forget Which Ones You Were Using.

BLOTTING PAGE

Use This Page To Prevent Marker Bleed Through. Or To Test And Keep Track Of Your Color Selections So You Can Pick Just The Right Colors Or Not Forget Which Ones You Were Using.

BLOTTING PAGE

Use This Page To Prevent Marker Bleed Through. Or To Test And Keep Track Of Your Color Selections So You Can Pick Just The Right Colors Or Not Forget Which Ones You Were Using.

BLOTTING PAGE

Use This Page To Prevent Marker Bleed Through. Or To Test And Keep Track Of Your Color Selections So You Can Pick Just The Right Colors Or Not Forget Which Ones You Were Using.

BLOTTING PAGE

Use This Page To Prevent Marker Bleed Through. Or To Test And Keep Track Of Your Color Selections So You Can Pick Just The Right Colors Or Not Forget Which Ones You Were Using.

BLOTTING PAGE

Use This Page To Prevent Marker Bleed Through. Or To Test And Keep Track Of Your Color Selections So You Can Pick Just The Right Colors Or Not Forget Which Ones You Were Using.

BLOTTING PAGE

Use This Page To Prevent Marker Bleed Through. Or To Test And Keep Track Of Your Color Selections So You Can Pick Just The Right Colors Or Not Forget Which Ones You Were Using.

BLOTTING PAGE

Use This Page To Prevent Marker Bleed Through. Or To Test And Keep Track Of Your Color Selections So You Can Pick Just The Right Colors Or Not Forget Which Ones You Were Using.

BLOTTING PAGE

Use This Page To Prevent Marker Bleed Through. Or To Test And Keep Track Of Your Color Selections So You Can Pick Just The Right Colors Or Not Forget Which Ones You Were Using.

BLOTTING PAGE

Use This Page To Prevent Marker Bleed Through. Or To Test And Keep Track Of Your Color Selections So You Can Pick Just The Right Colors Or Not Forget Which Ones You Were Using.

BLOTTING PAGE

Use This Page To Prevent Marker Bleed Through. Or To Test And Keep Track Of Your Color Selections So You Can Pick Just The Right Colors Or Not Forget Which Ones You Were Using.

BLOTTING PAGE

Use This Page To Prevent Marker Bleed Through. Or To Test And Keep Track Of Your Color Selections So You Can Pick Just The Right Colors Or Not Forget Which Ones You Were Using.

BLOTTING PAGE

Use This Page To Prevent Marker Bleed Through. Or To Test And Keep Track Of Your Color Selections So You Can Pick Just The Right Colors Or Not Forget Which Ones You Were Using.

BLOTTING PAGE

Use This Page To Prevent Marker Bleed Through. Or To Test And Keep Track Of Your Color Selections So You Can Pick Just The Right Colors Or Not Forget Which Ones You Were Using.

BLOTTING PAGE

Use This Page To Prevent Marker Bleed Through. Or To Test And Keep Track Of Your Color Selections So You Can Pick Just The Right Colors Or Not Forget Which Ones You Were Using.

BLOTTING PAGE

Use This Page To Prevent Marker Bleed Through. Or To Test And Keep Track Of Your Color Selections So You Can Pick Just The Right Colors Or Not Forget Which Ones You Were Using.

BLOTTING PAGE

Use This Page To Prevent Marker Bleed Through. Or To Test And Keep Track Of Your Color Selections So You Can Pick Just The Right Colors Or Not Forget Which Ones You Were Using.

BLOTTING PAGE

Use This Page To Prevent Marker Bleed Through. Or To Test And Keep Track Of Your Color Selections So You Can Pick Just The Right Colors Or Not Forget Which Ones You Were Using.

BLOTTING PAGE

Use This Page To Prevent Marker Bleed Through. Or To Test And Keep Track Of Your Color Selections So You Can Pick Just The Right Colors Or Not Forget Which Ones You Were Using.

BLOTTING PAGE

Use This Page To Prevent Marker Bleed Through. Or To Test And Keep Track Of Your Color Selections So You Can Pick Just The Right Colors Or Not Forget Which Ones You Were Using.

BLOTTING PAGE

Use This Page To Prevent Marker Bleed Through. Or To Test And Keep Track Of Your Color Selections So You Can Pick Just The Right Colors Or Not Forget Which Ones You Were Using.

www.ingramcontent.com/pod-product-compliance
Lightning Source LLC
Chambersburg PA
CBHW082340220526
45470CB00008B/2583